GITA ON THE GREEN

Gita on the Green

The Mystical Tradition
Behind *Bagger Vance*

Steven J. Rosen

Continuum
New York London

2000
The Continuum International Publishing Group Inc
370 Lexington Avenue, New York, NY 10017

The Continuum International Publishing Group Ltd
Wellington House, 125 Strand, London WC2R 0BB

Printed in the United States of America

To my friends who left too soon:
Steve Raskin, Paul Presti, Sal Caruso, Nirmala Devi,
Richard Dixon, Lohitaksha, and Hayagriva Prabhu.
May they find their Authentic Swing,
If they haven't found it already.

Contents

Acknowledgments

*M*any people have helped in the writing and publishing of this book, most prominent of whom are Alister Taylor, Joshua Greene, Madhusudana Das, Dhanurdhar Swami, Romapada Swami, Steven Rumbaugh, Mahamuni Prabhu, Vraja-kishor Prabhu, and Frank Oveis of Continuum. I would like especially to thank Tamal Krishna Goswami and Arvind Sharma for going over the manuscript. Their gracious and learned comments have enhanced the work in many ways.

My deepest appreciation, however, must go to my friend Chaturatma Das, for introducing me to Bagger Vance; to Steven Pressfield, for helping me develop my relationship with Vance and for writing a spirited and encouraging foreword; and most of all, to His Divine Grace A. C. Bhaktivedanta Swami Prabhupada, for giving me the insight with which to see the many correlations between Bagger Vance and Bhagavan Sri Krishna.

A Note about Sanskrit Pronunciation

I have purposely avoided the difficult-looking diacritical formations of Indic words and instead have replaced them with "user-friendly" phonetic spellings. The one exception involves words that begin with *jn-*, such as *jnana* and *jneya*. Such words are actually pronounced as if they were spelled with *gy-*, as *gyana* or *gyeya*. But Sanskrit specialists would look askance at such spellings, and so I have kept these words in their original forms, merely lifting off their diacritical marks for convenience and consistency.

Foreword

by Steven Pressfield
Author of *The Legend of Bagger Vance*

*O*ccasionally I'll be talking with someone who has read *The Legend of Bagger Vance* and he or she will ask, "Where did you get the idea?" I'm always delighted to answer. I tell them that the structure is modeled on the *Bhagavad-gita*. You have never seen eyes glaze over so fast. A guaranteed conversation stopper. I plunge on, however, explaining that the *Gita* is a Vedic scripture embedded in the larger epic, the *Mahabharata,* and that it tells the story of the warrior Arjuna, who receives spiritual instruction from his charioteer, Krishna, who happens to be God in human form. By the time I'm through, whoever I'm talking to has entered a state of advanced stupefaction.

So when the noted *Gita* scholar Steven Rosen phoned to declare his intention to write a book around the connections between *Bagger* and the text that inspired it, the first question out of my mouth was, "Are you sure?"

But Steve is the real deal as a *Gita* authority, about thirty years' worth, here and in India, and he had the bit firmly between his teeth. Thus this endeavor. Thus the book you hold in your hands.

What is the *Gita* anyway?

To call it a great work doesn't quite do it justice. If the universe were to be vaporized tomorrow and only one artifact had to stand to show what human beings had gleaned from their sojourn in earthly consciousness, one would be hard pressed to name something better than the *Gita.*

What I love is that it's not Western. It's not Jewish or Christian. Its message is not the eye-for-an-eye or turn-the-other-cheek with which we are familiar, but something from an entirely different quadrant of the compass.

The *Gita* appears to advocate violence. It states flatly that death does not exist. It calls absolute devotion essential to enlightenment. On one page it champions a hard-core warrior ethic; on another it declares harmlessness, *ahimsa,* the supreme virtue of God and humans. The *Gita* exhorts readers to action but admonishes that they have no right to the fruits of that action. Be a "lord of discipline," it urges, in the same breath commanding utter surrender to one's spiritual mentor.

It can be pretty daunting to us Westerners.

Which is where Steven Rosen's *Gita on the Green* comes in. Though Steve's focus in the past has been Sanskrit and theological texts, what makes his book exceptional is its accessibility. You can actually understand it! *Gita on the Green* takes *Bagger Vance* as a point of departure and launches from there into the source text at full strength. Steve's book is, as it should be, about the *Gita.* He uses golf and a novel about golf as levers to pry into that mighty husk of wisdom that has come to us from the sages of India.

One aspect of the *Gita* that has troubled Westerners is its seeming embrace of violence. I found Steven Rosen's perspective on this extremely enlightening. His take on *karma* and *dharma* is most edifying, as is the section on "the Field and the Knower." I never quite understood the concept of self-surrender until I read his pages on it. *Gita on the Green* addresses these most thorny kernels with a clarity of thought and expression that makes you say, "Ah! So that's what it's about!"

As Steven Rosen notes in his own introduction, there are eighteen chapters in the *Gita*, as there are eighteen holes in a round of golf. What he might be too modest to say is that he takes us out and back, illuminating not just the subtleties of this short par-four or the brilliance of that back-breaking five, but the way the holes build upon one another to form an entity greater than the sum of its parts, an expression that is at once profound, unified, and timeless.

Gita on the Green was a college education for me. I hope it will be for you.

Introduction

> In the East, men are not embarrassed to speak openly of the
> Self. But here in the West, such piety makes people uncom-
> fortable. That is where golf comes in.
>
> —Bagger Vance

*I*n researching this book, I found many unexpected
links between golf and Eastern mysticism. Some were
profound, even enlightening. Others were little more
than interesting fun facts. Perhaps the most intriguing of
these involves Vishnu, known in India as a manifestation of
Krishna, God, whose teachings I will soon discuss at length.
According to Bob Loeffelbein (author of *Offbeat Golf*),
Vishnu is, believe it or not, the "god of golf." In his book, he
explains that Vishnu is "responsible" for those distinct dim-
pled golf balls we now commonly associate with the game:

> Credit for the invention of the gutta-percha ball probably
> belongs to the Reverend Robert A. Paterson of St. Andrews,
> Scotland—with a bit of help from the Hindu god Vishnu. In
> 1848, Reverend Paterson received a package from India.
> Inside was a statue of Vishnu packed in gutta-percha—essen-
> tially a milky sap that hardens when molded. Seeking a sub-
> stitute for the feather-stuffed leather balls then in use, he

tried molding the gutta-percha into a golf ball. But, when he tried it out, this ball went flying every which way, until it developed some nicks in it. Then it flew fairly straight. These nicks ultimately became the modern-day dimples, which create air pressure under the ball and keep it afloat. Even a modern-day ball without dimples will drop quickly after 60 to 80 yards. (p. 148)

Gutta-percha soon became the standard for making golf balls. Thus, Vishnu gives a new dimension to the famous (if also humorous) definition of golf: It is a game in which a ball that is one-and-a-half inches in diameter is placed on another ball that is over eight thousand miles in diameter—with the object being to miss the big ball and hit the little one. Vishnu, it seems, is responsible for both balls.

There are many other lighthearted, interesting links between golf and the East, and I look at some of them in this book. For example, *Bhagavad-gita,* the Sanskrit religious classic known as the Bible of India, has eighteen chapters, and (coincidentally?) a round of golf has eighteen holes. While such parallels can be thought-provoking, this book primarily focuses on the deeper connections between golf and matters of the spirit, particularly as they relate to the teachings of *Bhagavad-gita.*

The Legend of Bagger Vance

In 1995, William Morrow and Company published *The Legend of Bagger Vance: Golf and the Game of Life,* a novel by Steven Pressfield that explores the spiritual side of golf. Although there have been several other works on golf and mysticism—including Michael Murphy's 1972 classic *Golf in the Kingdom,* which is considered the forerunner of the genre—Pressfield's book is unique. He creatively restructures *Bhagavad-gita,* originally spoken on a battlefield, so that it now takes place on a golf course. In his work, he introduces us to the mysterious caddie known as Bagger Vance (a variation on *Bhagavan,* "the Holy One," a Sanskrit name for Lord Sri Krishna, speaker of *Bhagavad-gita*), who knows the parallels between the secrets of golf and the secrets of life.

The setting of the novel revolves around a golf tournament at Krewe Island, off Savannah, Georgia's windy Atlantic shore. The year is 1931, and we are transported into an impending thirty-six-hole match. Bobby Jones and Walter Hagen, legends of golf in their own time, are joined by a reluctant opponent, the famed but troubled war hero Rannulph Junah (read: R. Junah, or Arjuna, Krishna's archer-devotee from *Bhagavad-gita*). The outcome of the game, as we soon see, is more dependent on Bagger Vance, a caddie who carries the secret of "the Authentic Swing," than on the talents of the golfers. Vance's inscrutable wisdom and mysterious powers guide the play and leave a lasting impression, not only on R. Junah but—sixty years later—on a brilliant but discouraged young medical student. The narrator of the story, Dr. Hardison Greaves (who parallels Sanjaya, the narrator of the *Gita*), was ten years old when he witnessed the epic golf battle in 1931. Today he shares Vance's knowledge with that medical student, and, through him, with each of us. The implication here is that, like the *Gita,* the instructions of Bagger Vance are not just for R. Junah, but for Everyman.

Bagger Vance, tall and blackish (like Krishna), turns the

game field into something more, into the battlefield of life. He instructs R. Junah in a good deal more than golf, and, by the end of the novel, it becomes clear that Bagger Vance is no ordinary mortal. ("Everything that is," says Vance, "is brought into being and sustained by me" [p. 184].)

Since the *Gita* is not mentioned directly (except in one verse, which opens the book), those who are unfamiliar with the ancient classic will not see it in Pressfield's novel. His work stands on its own. But for those who know the *Gita,* the parallels are uncanny. What I do in *Gita on the Green* is to make explicit that which is only implicit in Pressfield's work. I highlight the two books' many correlating sections, and in so doing, I hope, offer the reader a useful introduction to the *Bhagavad-gita.*

I spoke with Pressfield about why he wrote *Bagger Vance,* and he told me that he had always been interested in the *Gita* and appreciated the idea of Bhagavan, God, humbling Himself to become the charioteer of His devotee, Arjuna. In the same way, Pressfield said, a caddie, as qualified as he may be, takes the humble position of assisting the golfer.

In an interview published on the Bagger Vance website, Pressfield reveals his idea behind the book:

> The idea behind Bagger Vance was to do the *Bhagavad-gita* contemporarily. In the *Gita* the troubled warrior Arjuna receives instruction from Krishna, Supreme Lord of the Universe, who has assumed human form as Arjuna's charioteer. Instead of a troubled warrior, it's a troubled golf champion (Rannulph Junah); instead of his charioteer, it's his caddie— Bagger Vance. . . . Golf, as everyone knows who has played it and loved it, is a very mystical sport. A golf course is like a battlefield. It even looks like a battlefield, with its rolling ramparts and redoubts.

Bhagavad-gita
How to Approach the Game

It is clear from *Bagger Vance* that Pressfield has high regard for the *Gita,* generally interpreting it according to traditional models. The *Gita's* vastness and complexity allow for many possible readings, and all of them have merit. The ancient spiritual tradition from which the *Gita* emerges—called the Vaishnava tradition—explains what might be missed in a general reading of the *Gita:* that such texts are meant to be understood in certain esoteric lineages. The *Gita* itself says that "the message of the *Gita* should be heard in disciplic succession (*parampara*), for this is how saintly kings of bygone days understood the holy text" (4.2). Moreover, the *Gita* says that to truly imbibe its internal message, one must be a "devotee and friend" of Lord Krishna (*bhakto 'si me sakha cheti,* 4.3). These criteria need not be as intimidating as they at first sound: There are English editions of the *Gita* available today that accurately represent the disciplic conclusions. And being Krishna's "devotee and friend," according to the tradition itself, can (in addition to its literal reading) be interpreted as "giving faithful aural reception" to the message of the *Gita*—in other words, to approach it with an open mind.

While Pressfield's use of the *Gita* may seem a bit unorthodox, there is much to suggest that he is, to a significant degree, Krishna's "devotee and friend." That is to say, his use of the *Gita* is in good spirit and with an obvious respect for its teachings. Of course, the "lineage" factor is important—without the benefit of a teacher in disciplic succession, it is difficult to get all the *Gita* has to offer.

His Divine Grace A. C. Bhaktivedanta Swami Prabhupada (1896–1977), author of *Bhagavad-gita As It Is* and one
of the world's leading authorities on the Vaishnava tradition, discusses this principle of disciplic succession in his
commentary on the *Gita,*

> This is the mystery of the disciplic succession. When the spir-
> itual master is bona fide, then one can hear *Bhagavad-gita*
> directly, as Arjuna heard it. . . . If one does not come in dis-
> ciplic succession, he cannot hear Krishna; therefore, his
> knowledge is always imperfect, at least as far as under-
> standing *Bhagavad-gita* is concerned. (*Bhagavad-gita As It Is,*
> 18.75, purport)

In his commentary on the Upanishads (*Ishopanishad,*
Mantra 13), Prabhupada writes:

> When Lord Sri Krishna was present on this earth, the bhakti-
> yoga principles defined in the *Bhagavad-gita* had become
> distorted; therefore, the Lord had to reestablish the disciplic
> system beginning with Arjuna, who was the most confiden-
> tial friend and devotee of the Lord. The Lord clearly told
> Arjuna (Bg. 4.3) that it was because Arjuna was His devotee
> and friend that he could understand the principles of the
> *Bhagavad-gita.* In other words, only the Lord's devotee and
> friend can understand the *Gita.* This also means that only
> one who follows the path of Arjuna can understand the
> *Bhagavad-gita.* . . . At the present moment there are many
> interpreters and translators of this sublime dialogue who . . .
> explain the verses of the *Bhagavad-gita* in their own way. . . .
> Such interpreters believe neither in Sri Krishna nor in His
> eternal abode. How, then, can they explain *Bhagavad-gita?*

The Legend of Bagger Vance is not exactly what Prabhupada is writing about here. It is not a formal commentary

on the *Gita,* nor is it a direct statement on Krishna's teachings. Rather, it is a well-written work of fiction with many *Gita*-inspired themes and ideas. In this respect, the book is quite successful: it is an engaging read with intimations of the Divine. Naturally, differences between the *Gita* and *Bagger Vance* are inevitable, and some of these will be explored throughout this work. But the correlations between these two books far outnumber the differences, and, as we shall see, lead to quite creative and interesting perceptions of metaphysical truth. Overall, Pressfield's book renders a valuable service—it places the spirit of the *Gita* on a new playing field.

———— Bagger and Bhagavan: The Links ————

Imagine, if you will, Junah and Arjuna meeting at the links, discussing the parallels in their respective books while tackling the green. They might each begin their discussion by relating their most intense moment of turmoil, when they first became aware of the seemingly senseless battle that lay before them. In the Bagger Vance story, for example, the grief-stricken Junah sees the galleries gathering like armies before the match. He becomes overwhelmed with depression, ordering Bagger to drive the Chalmers out onto the dunes between "the armies." Once in that strategic position, he pulls over, lays down his clubs, and refuses to participate in the match.

As elaborated upon in the thirteenth chapter of *Bagger Vance:*

> "Put the clubs away . . . ," he [Junah] said in a voice nearly inaudible. "I see no profit in them or this whole fool enterprise."

"Your mind is clearly in torment, Junah," Bagger Vance spoke slowly and evenly. "Tell me please: what is the nature of your complaint?"

Junah glanced up sharply at this word, which seemed to trivialize his emotion. "It couldn't be more obvious, could it?" He gestured toward the multitudes in their bright battle lines, visible across the linksland. "This whole endeavor is a freak show. A joke. What good will any of it do me, or anyone attached to it?" (p. 94)

Junah's hands were trembling. He ran them in pain through his hair, eyes gazing hollowly before him into the dunes "What is ever gained by 'defeating' others? What can be gained here today? If I win I take no pleasure, and if I lose . . . ." (p. 95)

This correlates precisely to the first chapter of the *Gita:*

Arjuna said: O infallible Krishna, please draw my chariot between the two armies—I want to see who is present here, who is desirous of fighting, and with whom I must contend in this great battle. (1.21–22)

Sanjaya, the narrator, said: Being thus addressed by Arjuna, Lord Krishna drew up the magnificent chariot in the midst of both armies. (1.24)

At this point Arjuna could see that among the armies were his fathers, grandfathers, teachers, maternal uncles, brothers, sons, grandsons, friends, and also his father-in-law and well-wishers—all were present there. (1.26)

Arjuna said: My dear Krishna, seeing my friends and relatives present before me in such a fighting mood, I feel the limbs of my body quivering and my mouth drying up. In fact, my whole body is trembling, and my hair is standing on end. My bow is slipping from my hand, and my skin is burning. (1.28–29)

O Govinda [Krishna], of what avail to us are kingdoms, happiness, or even life itself when all those for whom we may desire them are now ready to engage in combat? O Krishna, seeing all my relatives ready to give up their lives and properties as they stand before me, why should I wish to kill them, even if I were to survive? O maintainer of all living beings, I am not prepared to fight with them even in exchange for the universe, let alone this earth. (1.32–35)

If Junah and Arjuna were to continue this fictitious dialogue, they would inevitably discuss the point in their lives when they desperately sought help from their respective mentors.

For example, while Junah is besieged by what can only be called an existential dilemma, Vance helps him understand his true identity, much as Krishna reminds Arjuna that he is the soul rather than the body:

"Tell me who you are Junah. Who, in your deepest parts, when all that is inauthentic has been stripped away. Are you your name, Rannulph Junah? Will that hit this shot for you? Are you your illustrious forebears? Will they hit it? . . . Are you your roles, Junah? Scion, soldier, Southerner? Husband, father, lover? Slayer of the foe in battle, comforter of the friend at home? Are you your virtues, Junah, or your sins? Your deeds, your feats? Are you your dreams or your nightmares? Tell me, Junah. Can you hit the ball with any of these?" . . . Vance pressed yet harder, "Then who are you? Answer me!" (p. 113)

Bagger Vance elaborates on the spiritual dimension of reality, and that all beings partake of this higher nature.

Gita parallels go further. Though Bagger Vance doesn't use Sanskrit terminology, he offers a brilliant analogy involving the path of discipline (Karma-yoga), the path of knowledge (Jnana-yoga), and the path of devotion (Bhakti-yoga), acknowledging the supremacy of *bhakti* over all others. While explaining how to master the Game, Vance describes three possible approaches:

> The first path, I heard him say, was the path of Discipline. It had something to do with beating balls, with endless practice, an utter relentless commitment to achieving physical mastery of the game.
>
> Second was the path of Wisdom. I heard practically nothing of what Vance said here (I was checking yardage to three separate bunkers off the eighteenth) except, I believe, that the process was largely mental—a study of the Swing much like a scientist might undertake: analysis, dissection, and so on.
>
> Third (and this I heard most of) was the path of love.
>
> On this path, Vance said, we learn the Swing the way a child acquires its native tongue. We absorb it through pure love of the game. This is how boys and girls learn, intuitively, through their pores, by total devotion and immersion. Without technically "studying" the swing, they imbibe it by osmosis, from watching accomplished players and from sensing it within their own bones. (pp. 73–74)

Vance goes on to explain that the path of love is the most effective. If you love the Game, you have the best chance of being a great player.

In the *Gita*, Krishna reveals His Godhood to Arjuna by giving him the ability to see "a cosmic form," or a vision in which the great prince inexplicably sees "everything—moving and nonmoving—completely, in one place" (11.7). Vance also shows Junah a universal form: "Only to you, Junah, will I show myself in all my power. I give you the divine eye with which to see; otherwise the merest fragment of this vision would be your end" (p. 176). He proceeds to show Junah a form that approximates Arjuna's vision in the Gita. Arjuna, by the way, is also given "divine eyes" so that he may witness the revelation (11.8).

Vance identifies himself with all-devouring time (p. 186), as Krishna does in the *Gita* (11.32). And there are several other parallels along these same lines. Finally, Vance says, "I come again in every age, taking on human form to perform the duty I set myself. I return to right the balance of things" (p. 184). This directly correlates with Krishna's revelation in the Gita: "I Myself appear, again and again in every age, to liberate the pious and to annihilate the evildoers, as well as to reestablish the principles of religion" (4.8).

Junah and Arjuna no doubt have a lot in common, and if they were to discuss their stories further, many of the parallels I address in this book would be the subject of their conversation.

Pop Goes the *Gita*

Throughout the *Bagger Vance* book, Vance describes the search for the "Authentic Swing," which, he says, is actually the search for "the Self." In promoting the pursuit of self-realization, Pressfield's book transcends the usual limitations of novels, and it can well inspire readers in the spiritual quest. While the book may or may not actually help us find our Authentic Swing, the author contributes to our game in a major way, encouraging us to have more than a fling with our Swing. Judging by the popularity of the newly released paperback edition (Avon Books), many readers will be swinging from bookstores to movie theaters.

Bhagavad-gita, The Movie? Well, not exactly. The *Gita* has been adapted for pop culture over the years—mainly out of India—in terms of popular movies, musicals, and the performing arts. As of the writing of this work, *The Legend of Bagger Vance* is being made into a film. But don't expect to learn *Bhagavad-gita* from the movie. If the *Bagger Vance* book is a few golf holes short of the *Gita,* the movie is on another playing field altogether. The *Gita*-like mysticism is snuffed out of the Bagger Vance character, and he appears like a mere trickster instead—the wise one is replaced with a wise guy.

Nonetheless, people in the know are saying that this will be among the blockbuster movies of the year. Critics are even now, before its release, calling it "a major hole in one." But for the real deal behind the Bagger Vance story, one would do well to go to the source—*Bhagavad-gita*—the original. For the *Gita,* it might be said, is "the Holy One's hole in one."

How I became interested in the *Gita* and exactly how Bagger Vance relates to this best of books, is the subject of this present work.

My Search for
"the Authentic Swing"

> It don't mean a thing
> If it ain't got that swing.
> —Duke Ellington

*T*he *Legend of Bagger Vance* is essentially about the search for "the Authentic Swing." This is golfspeak for self-realization—the pursuit of the true Self on an intimate, personal level. Everyone must find the "swing" that suits him or her best, Vance teaches us, and when one does, one finds that one is in touch with one's own soul and with the essence of the universe, with God. According to Bagger Vance, finding the Authentic Swing is the purpose of life—it is tantamount to finding one's truest essence:

"Consider the swing itself," he said. "It's existence metaphysically, I mean. It has no objective reality of its own, no existence at all save when our bodies create it, and yet who can deny that it exists, independently of our bodies, as if on another plane of reality."

"Am I hearing you right sir? . . . Are you equating the swing with the soul, with the Authentic Soul?"

"I prefer the word *Self*," Bagger Vance said. "The Authentic Self. I believe this is the reason for the endless fascination of golf. The game is a metaphor for the soul's search for its true ground and identity. . . . The search for the Authentic Swing is a parallel to the search for the Self." (pp. 69–70)

I have always been a truth seeker. In my experience, this is different from being a golfer—although some equate the two. The rather obvious difference is nicely articulated by golf pro and Catholic priest Mike Lander, who writes in his book *Play It as It Lies: Golf and the Spiritual Life:*

> I don't believe that proficiency in golf is synonymous with spiritual advancement. If that were true, then Jack Nicklaus, easily the best player of this century, would also be the most spiritually aware person of his time. Maybe he is. Everything I've read about him indicates that he is as gracious and generous as he is capable of playing the game. But I'd probably have to give the nod to someone like the Dalai Lama, and *he* plays to a twenty-six handicap. (pp. 1–2)

For some, I guess, enlightenment can come on a golf course, especially if they have someone like Bagger Vance to give them guidance. I was not so lucky.

My search for the Authentic Swing took me to India when I was a teenager. Like many children of the sixties, I became obsessed with truth and believed I could find it only in the East. So I went to the land of the Ganges.

Bagger Vance, too, says that he journeyed the subcontinent:

> "You've been to India, Sir?"
> "Many times," Bagger Vance replied. (p. 70)

Did Vance have an opportunity to explore India's many golf links? We may never know. By all accounts, he would have enjoyed it. Professor Ed Dimock, a prominent authority on Bengali Vaishnavism, writes about the Indian green in his book *Mr. Dimock Explores the Mysteries of the East:*

Playing golf in India is, in its essentials, not very different from playing golf elsewhere. There are, of course, minor differences: little temples and tombs of saints in the middle of the fairways, cobras in the rough, and I am told that if you overshoot the ninth green on the "highest golf course in the world," in Darjeeling, your ball plunges four hundred feet into a clear glacial stream that carries it to Bangladesh. (p. 102)

Somehow, while in India, I missed the whole golf connection. However, I did meet a holy person who nurtured in me a desire to pursue ultimate reality. He didn't play golf. Several years later, on the BMT subway in New York, a Hare Krishna devotee gave me a copy of the *Bhagavad-gita*. This also inspired my search for truth. He, too, was not a golfer. Nonetheless, I would like to relate both stories as a backdrop to my comparative analysis of the *Bhagavad-gita* and *Bagger Vance.*

Swinging in India

In 1972, as a truth-seeking seventeen-year-old, I took time off from high school (much to my mother's disappointment) and set out for India. My goal was simple: I wanted to find the Ultimate Unity of Existence, that mystical form of the Cosmos who is known by some as the Indwelling Lord of all. I had been reading ancient Vedic (Indian) texts in translation, studying Sanskrit, *yoga*, and Vedanta. This culminated in a need to know the beautiful truth—the ultimate Oneness—that lay at the core of existence. I was tired of just reading about it in books. Having imagined in my mind's eye what it would be like to "perceive the truth" and to meet sages who had actually realized it, I became certain that a simple trip to the homeland of Buddha and Krishna would afford me instant enlightenment—or at least a pointer in the right direction. My plan was to meet holy men in Benares, Vrindavan, Jagannath Puri, and Mayapur—places that, through my reading, I had come to revere as more holy than my native Brooklyn.

The plane landed in Delhi. It was the middle of a dark night. I found myself in the midst of countless eyes that were darker still. Smoke seemed to cover everything except those dark eyes. The heat was nearly unbearable, but I was excited—excited and scared. Here I was, in a place that most seekers from the West only dream about. And it actually seemed like a dream. But I was there: Stranger in a strange land. Questions filled my head. Where am I? Why am I here? Am I crazy? I'm in a Third World country. No one to turn to. Dismal poverty. And yet—it's a land of sages. Hidden truth. Spiritual wealth.

After arriving by taxi in Vrindavan, which was my first important stop, I met a *sadhu,* a holy person, whose name was Krishnadas. He was sitting on the waves (!) of the Yamuna River, mystically balancing himself on four huge lotus leaves. Seeing my amazement, he gently raised himself off the leaves and invited me to sit on them in his place. As he rose from his seat, the leaves started to naturally float apart. He then gently brought them back together with his hands, and, miraculously, they stayed in position as he placed them on the water. He again gestured to me, saying with his hands and smile that I should sit on the leaves, balancing on the water as he had done.

Trying to sit on the leaves as if I were an expert *yogi,* I quickly came crashing down into the holy Yamuna waters.

The *sadhu* laughed joyously as he watched me make my big splash as a seeker of truth. We became quick friends, and so, after about one week, I decided to ask him about the One Reality, the God of sages, after which (or after Whom) I was so eagerly searching. He shook his head disapprovingly. He said, with his heavy Bengali accent, that the Truth had to be realized, and that realization comes from *sadhana*, or spiritual practices. Questions and answers can help, he said, but ultimately it was necessary to purify my lifestyle if I wanted to perceive the Truth.

So in the weeks that followed I adopted a traditional monklike lifestyle: a vegetarian diet, celibacy, and avoidance of gambling and intoxication. Most of all, I spent many hours chanting Vedic mantras, visiting long-established shrines, and performing menial service for the holy men and women who had dedicated their lives to the Absolute. It was a hard life for a true-blue Westerner like me, but not one that I was entirely unaccustomed to. In my years as a seeker, I had, from time to time, engaged in many if not all of these austerities. But here it was a little more difficult, without the material amenities afforded by the West. Still, I was determined to make my best and most sincere effort, taking full advantage of my time with genuine *sadhus*.

Tee for Two

One day Krishnadas turned to me and said, "You know, of course, that the One Reality is actually Two: Radha and Krishna. God has both female and male dimensions—these Two, complete in themselves, constitute the One Absolute Truth." I was stunned. The Upanishads speak of One

Absolute Truth, the Brahman. Other parts of the Vedic literature and certainly latter-day Hindu tradition speak of the
incarnations of Godhead and, sure, there are allusions to
"the One becoming Many." But I thought that this referred
to how the One Supreme Truth—God, as we say in the West—
becomes all the many living beings. I thought it referred to
our own individual divinity.

I immediately broached the subject of the One becoming
Many, telling him my long-held belief that we are all God in
our own way. He looked at me as if he had just eaten a rot-
ten egg. "Absolutely not," he said. "It is true that the One
becomes Many, but that is a different thing. The 'many' are
such removed expansions that they are considered only
part and parcel of Him. They are one with Him in quality,
but not in quantity." Krishnadas decided to make this
clearer by using an analogy: "The ocean, when chemically
analyzed, is the same as a drop of water. But the ocean is
great, while the drop of water is tiny. Similarly, the Ultimate
Reality has full strength, beauty, wealth, fame, knowledge,
bliss, and so on. We have these same qualities, but in minute
proportion. God is great, and we are small."

I was confused. At least India recognized many gods, I
thought. Maybe this had something to do with "the One
becoming Many." So I decided to ask him about the Hindu
pantheon, about India's many gods and goddesses—Shiva,
Brahma, Indra, Ganesh, Kali, Durga, and so on. He
responded that God is one, but that He has many angels, or
helpers. The other gods are merely demigods, or "partial"
gods, he said. They are highly empowered beings who assist
the Lord in universal affairs. He assured me that, contrary
to popular belief, true Indian religion was monotheistic, just

as adamant about God's uniqueness as any of the Western religious traditions.

Krishnadas looked tired. I decided to let the subject rest until the next day. Besides, when he brought up the ocean analogy, it made me think of the time I fell in the Yamuna. I could still see him laughing. My ego was still bruised from the fall.

By the time the sun rose, we had long since arisen ourselves, offering oblations to many manifestations of Godhead with ancient Vedic mantras. These manifestations were clearly different from the demigods we had spoken about on the previous day. We were chanting Vishnu's various names and those of Nrisimha, Vamana, Rama, and Varaha, among others. "Krishnadas Prabhu," I ventured slowly, "do these various manifestations of the Supreme have anything to do with Radha and Krishna?" He smiled enthusiastically. "Yes," he said, "they are all expansions and incarnations of Radha and Krishna. They are above the demigods, nondifferent from Krishna. But make no mistake: Radha and Krishna are the source. They are the original Personalities of Godhead."

Ah! Now, I thought, I am getting somewhere. I was beginning to understand. I tried to show my powerful reasoning capabilities: "So Radha and Krishna are the source of these manifestations," I said to him with growing confidence, "just like the One Supreme Reality is the source of Radha and Krishna."

"No!" he slammed his hand down for emphasis. "Radha and Krishna exist eternally, and the 'One Reality' is simply an inferior, impersonal manifestation of Radha and Krishna. If you study our Indian scriptures closely, you'll see that the One is not really One, but it is Two." His words struck me like a ton of bricks. Here I was in India, halfway around the world, looking for the ultimate One Reality—and now I'm being told that the One is ultimately Two!

I asked him to please elaborate. This he did, using logic, reason, and showing me numerous scriptural texts to support his case. "You see," he began, "there are three levels of God realization described in the *Vedas*: Brahman, Paramatma, and Bhagavan. Basically, these three levels manifest gradually to the practitioner of *yoga*. Brahman is fundamental, an impersonal realization about the Ultimate Oneness of existence. Superior to that is Paramatma realization, where one sees that Oneness as a localized Lord, the Supersoul, who permeates all of creation—He is within every atom and within everyone's heart. Finally, there is Bhagavan, wherein one realizes the Supreme Personality of Godhead, Krishna, who is Bhagavan Himself. Now, at the height of Bhagavan realization, one realizes that Bhagavan has male and female attributes, the original forms of which are called Krishna and Radha."

"Can you explain these three levels of God realization more clearly, Krishnadas?"

"I'll give you an analogy," he said. "The three stages are like seeing a hillside from a distance. The all-pervasive and impersonal Brahman is like seeing the hill from very far away—it is misty, and variegatedness is imperceptible. As one gets closer to the hill, one is able to make out more clearly various forms. He may even see that the green hill is in fact made up of many trees. This is comparable to Paramatma realization, where one begins to perceive divine personality. As one gets closer still, one can see all the different forms on the hillside and perhaps even meet the people who live there. This is Bhagavan realization, wherein one meets the Lord and His associates." He added that the cultivation of *jnana,* or knowledge, usually leads one to the impersonalistic path; *yoga,* he said, generally takes one to Paramatma realization; and *bhakti,* or devotional love, leads to realization of Bhagavan, of Radha and Krishna.

I needed to know more. "Please tell me," I said, "are Radha and Krishna absolutely different? Are they two distinct personalities?" He seemed to like this question and decided to elaborate: "Radha and Krishna are one and the same, but they exist in two separate bodies. In this way, the One Supreme Truth enjoys *rasa,* or 'relationship,' tasting the bliss of loving Himself. He wants to taste the love that His dearest devotees have for Him." As he spoke, I began to understand what he was saying, at least intellectually. Krishnadas was explaining that Radha and Krishna are the "One" after which I was searching, but that they exist as Two in order to relish loving exchange. This They do with each other and with Their unlimited number of pure devotees.

——— Sri Chaitanya: The Volcano of Love ———

I felt there was something more that Krishnadas was not telling me. I took a wild shot: "Do the Two ever become One again?" His eyes opened wide with surprise, and he visibly looked as though a wave of ecstasy engulfed his body. "Yes! Yes!" he said. "This is Chaitanya Mahaprabhu! Radha and Krishna in one body. This is the most confidential part of the Vedic literature. The male and female Absolute—the Two become One again, embodying one divine form. This creates an unworkable situation—an explosion—giving way to divine madness."

"What do you mean?" I asked him, with an uncontrollable thirst to hear more.

"The ecstasy of their diverse emotions and the interaction of their love for each other cannot be contained in a single form," he said, now with eyes closed so he could relish the reality about which he spoke, "and so Chaitanya has been described as a volcano of divine love, erupting with the lava of spiritual madness. This transcendental explosion is the great mystery of the Two becoming One again, and it is revealed and discussed only among the most advanced *yogi*s."

My mind was reeling. I started to think in Western terms. Male and female in one body? It brought to mind one of Plato's conceptions, preserved in his *Republic*, that the original human condition involved "both sexes in one body." He called it "androgyny." Similar ideas were echoed more than twelve centuries after Plato when Edgar Cayce explored Atlantean legends. And today the conception has been developed further by Mircea Eliade, who created the term *coincidentia oppositorum* ("the residing of opposites in the same object"). I shared these thoughts with Krishnadas, but he was unimpressed. After all, it had all been discussed long ago in the Vedic literature. Besides, the Western idea was just a vague derivative, a sort of perverted reflection that is full of materialistic misconceptions and unwholesome half-truths.

"Can you tell me more about Chaitanya," I asked him.

"He appeared in India only five hundred years ago," Krishnadas said, "but the highest self-realized souls all knew Him as Radha and Krishna combined. He came in the guise of His own devotee. You see, before incarnating as Mahaprabhu," Krishnadas continued, "Krishna thought deeply about the virtues of Radha, about how deeply She loves Him, and about the ecstasy She feels as His most intimate servitor. Wanting to experience these emotions Himself, Krishna decides to incarnate by assuming certain of His own features and certain features of both the emotions and body of Radha. For example, Chaitanya exhibits the mood, disposition, and golden color of Radha, though He takes on a male body like that of Krishna. This combined manifestation, when reflected upon with the guidance of pure devotees, can bring one to the highest conception of the Absolute Truth. The countless pages of Vedic literature and millennia of sages discussing Indian philosophy are nothing more than an arrow pointing in this direction."

"Krishna is the enchanter of the world," Krishnadas concluded, "but Radha enchants even Krishna. Her enchanting abilities are the most bewildering thing in God's creation, placing even Krishna under their powerful spell. Krishna's ability to enter the magical realm of Radha's love is called 'Chaitanya,' and this principle is embodied in the form of Sri Chaitanya, who walked the earth with His most intimate devotees. Chaitanya Mahaprabhu, in manifest form, then, represents the reality that Radha and Krishna are One. Just as musk and its scent are not divided, much like fire and flame, so Radha and Krishna are the ultimate One Supreme Truth. This dual and simultaneously nondual nature of reality is the greatest secret of all and is embodied in Chaitanya Mahaprabhu's appearance in this world."

Soon after this incident, I had to bid farewell to Krishnadas, and so I went to Benares and the other holy places I had initially planned to visit. My whole trip in India lasted a total of three months, though it seemed like an eternity. Eventually, I realized that I was young, and that although my stay in India was invaluable, I had to get back to "the real world." Regarding Krishnadas, I soon met various holy men who expressed in diverse ways the same truths I had learned from him—and many even attempted to refute Krishnadas's profound understanding of Indian religion. But I never quite thought of the One Supreme Being in the same way again. I guess Krishnadas had quite an effect on me. His explanation of ultimate reality and Indian philosophy was really more than I could accommodate at the time. Truth be told, it's more than I can accommodate now! But it left a deep impression, and, then as now, it rings true. I can still see his emotional eyes as he spoke to me about the One becoming Two, and then becoming One again. His enthusiasm was contagious, as were his devotion, blissfulness, and his whole mystical demeanor. And yet, whenever I approach a large body of water, I think about our first meeting, when he sat on the large lotus leaves, magically balancing on the waves of the river. And I think about the time I fell in. This reminds me that I am not Krishnadas and I do not have the realization and insight into reality that he has. But I *do* know that he saw something, or someone, on another plane of existence. He had certainly found his Authentic Swing.

Bhagavad-gita "As It Is"

About one year later, I was on my way to school (I had dropped out to go to India, and now I had to make up for "lost time")—New York's High School of Art and Design— and happened upon a copy of *Bhagavad-gita*, a battered Penguin paperback. I had of course been introduced to the

Gita much earlier, even before my trip to India. But now, after visiting the land of the *Gita*'s birth, I was especially intrigued. I really couldn't make heads or tails of the message, but I appreciated that it was some sort of spiritual philosophy and was written with great poetic style.

I decided to look up "Bhagavad-gita" in *Webster's Unabridged Dictionary:* "A philosophical poem relating a discourse between Krishna (God) and a warrior, Arjuna; it is a sacred Hindu text." I was interested in pursuing this. It was reminiscent of what I had learned from Krishnadas.

In my last year of high school, I rummaged through old bookstores, looking for different editions of *Bhagavad-gita.* Some editions were versified translations, some were prose. All were alluring, and all were mysterious. The *Gita,* it seemed, was a book of inscrutable wisdom, of contradictory truths. Was it, for instance, a glorification of war, or a treatise on nonviolence? Was it allegory, or was it to be taken literally?

Although my friends and I were reading Hesse, Castañeda, Buber, Tillich, and many other popular existentialist writers of the time, I maintained a special fascination for the *Gita.* Most editions seemed to relegate Krishna's personality to the background, emphasizing instead the impersonal Brahman—God's monistic feature. These translators, I thought, would have done well to spend a few days with Krishnadas.

Then, just prior to entering college, I picked up a copy of *Bhagavad-gita As It Is,* by His Divine Grace A. C. Bhaktivedanta Swami Prabhupada, the founder and spiritual master of the International Society for Krishna Consciousness. Here was a refreshing change. Srila Prabhupada did not explain the *Gita* in a metaphorical or analogical way.

His approach was literal—much in the style and tradition of Krishnadas—giving the essential message of each text according to the ancient Vaishnava understanding.

I remember the day I received *Bhagavad-gita As It Is* as if it were yesterday, although it was about twenty-six years ago. I was on the train on my way home from school. I was reading a popular translation of the *Gita* when a Hare Krishna devotee approached me. He was asking for donations, and he was selling, of all things, copies of *Bhagavad-gita As It Is*, Srila Prabhupada's *Gita*. I was skeptical of Westerners dressed like Indian *sadhus*, but I thought I would give him a chance.

I'll always remember what that bold Hare Krishna monk said to me: "You're reading poison!" he exclaimed. I was shocked. I knew little about the Hare Krishna movement, but I knew they were Indophiles, of sorts. At least I knew that they had high regard for the *Gita* and its message of devotion to Krishna.

"The *Gita* is as pure as milk," he continued, "but even milk becomes poison when touched by the lips of a serpent." Although I felt his criticism a bit extreme, I could understand that his reservations were with the particular translation I was reading and not with the *Gita* itself. I also had misgivings about this particular edition, as only the first six chapters were translated. Why would the translator leave out the remaining twelve chapters? Agreeing with the devotee that something was amiss, I accepted a copy of *Bhagavad-gita As It Is*, which he gave me free.

Srila Prabhupada's *Gita* was precisely what I was looking for. Unlike other editions, it provided me with a clear understanding of the personalities involved and of the entire story behind the work. The *Gita*'s almost simple message became apparent: surrender to God, develop love for Krishna. This same conclusion was no doubt there in other translations— I mean, it is there in the *Gita* itself—but somehow Prabhupada's version made it clear, as if his was a transparent glass while others were tinted. It seemed that many other modern translators and commentators were inadvertently covering the essence, not seeing the Authentic Swing for the Inauthentic Field, as it were.

But I wanted to be certain. And after I enrolled in Queens College that fall, I took a course in Sanskrit. Now I would be able to compare translations. I learned that most scholars agreed with Prabhupada, praising his work as the definitive *Bhagavad-gita* from a devotional point of view. And his particular edition was read and accepted worldwide. His books were in 75 percent of America's college and university libraries and were sometimes used as course material and supplementary reading in philosophy, religion, literature, and Asian studies. Dr. Rasik Vihari Joshi, chairman of the department of Sanskrit at the University of Delhi, had said, "Indian religion and Indology will both forever remain indebted to Srila Prabhupada for making Vaishnava thought and philosophy available around the world through his translations of and commentaries on *Bhagavad-gita* and *Srimad Bhagavatam*. Words fail to express my joy and appreciation for these excellent editions." Similarly, Dr. Samuel D. Atkins, professor of Sanskrit at Princeton University, wrote, "I am most impressed with A. C. Bhaktivedanta Swami Prabhupada's scholarly and authoritative edition of *Bhagavad-gita*. It is a most valuable work for the scholar as well as the layman and of great utility as a reference book as well as a textbook."

There are those who dismiss Prabhupada's work as well.

Clearly, there are scholars who feel that Prabhupada unduly emphasizes the devotional approach. They say that he translates with the agenda of a practitioner, reading Vaishnava teachings into a text that doesn't necessarily call for it. After studying many different *Gitas*, I must say that different versions seem to serve different purposes. There are editions that are true to the Sanskrit letter, and those that are true to the spirit; there are scholarly translations and devotional ones. The *Gita*, however, is primarily a text on *bhakti*, or devotion to Krishna. Thus, editions capturing its devotional component would be more authentic, more representative of what the text originally intended to say.

Srila Prabhupada's *Bhagavad-gita As It Is*, I was learning, stands as a challenge to all armchair philosophers who depart from the *Gita*'s central teaching of devotional service to the supreme Lord Krishna. Even Mahatma Gandhi, his dedication notwithstanding, offered the world only a metaphorical interpretation of the *Gita*, for in this way he sought to authorize and popularize his philosophy of *satya-graha*, passive resistance. Gandhi's work emphasizes *karma* (action) as opposed to *bhakti*.

——— Action, Knowledge, and Devotion ———

A. L. Herman, professor of philosophy at the University of Wisconsin-Stevens Point, wrote an interesting book called *A Brief Introduction to Hinduism*. In this work he divides the *Gita*'s essential teaching into the three subdivisions of *karma* (action), *jnana* (knowledge), and *bhakti* (devotion). Further, he shows how these three approaches to the *Gita* are best represented by the translations and commentaries of three twentieth-century thinkers: Gandhi for *karma,* Ramana Maharshi for *jnana,* and Prabhupada for *bhakti.* Since, again, the *Gita* is essentially a work that focuses on *bhakti,* I will use Prabhupada's *Gita* as my main reference throughout this book, though the translations are my own.

Ever since Charles Wilkins first translated the *Bhagavad-gita* into English in 1785, there have been literally hundreds of translations. Before 1968, however, when Srila Prabhupada released his *Bhagavad-gita As It Is,* few Westerners had become devotees of Krishna. It seems that, prior to Prabhupada, Westerners, for the most part, misunderstood the central point of the *Gita:* "Always be conscious of Me and become My devotee. Worship Me and offer your praise unto Me. In this way you will definitely come to Me in the end. I promise you this because you are My dear friend" (18.65). Or, more directly, "I can only be understood in truth, as I am, by the path of *bhakti*" (18.55).

In the *Gita,* Krishna tells Arjuna to surrender to Him in love and devotion. The *Gita* makes careful record of the fact that it is not metaphorical by using the words *krishna saksha kahayah svayam* (18.75). These words clearly indicate that Krishna was directly (*saksha*) in front of Arjuna, personally (*svayam*) explaining these ideas to him—much as Vance was right there with R. Junah and as Krishnadas stood in front of me.

By 1975 I was convinced that I had found an "authentic" *Bhagavad-gita*—I was studying in "disciplic succession," as the *Gita* itself says one should—and that through this, along with what I had learned from Krishnadas, I would one day find my Authentic Swing, that is, I would realize my essential nature and gradually develop love of God. Alas, I am still working on that Swing. It is, no doubt, a lifelong affair.

But certain things have become clear. My studies of the *Gita* reveal that it basically deals with three subjects in detail: (1) *karma*, (2) *jnana*, and (3) *bhakti*. Thus, in this book, I will explore these three phenomena—and how knowledge of these things can have an impact on one's life. I will also look at how they are dealt with, or not dealt with, in *Bagger Vance*.

Before doing so, however, I would like to address the issue of violence in the *Bhagavad-gita*. There are those who deny the value of the *Gita* and its teachings merely because it takes place on a battlefield. Perhaps such readers would prefer that Krishna spoke to Arjuna on a golf course, peaceful and serene.

I, too, was taken aback when I first discovered that Arjuna was a warrior and that Krishna delivered His message at the onset of a devastating battle. It seemed hypocritical, I felt, to speak of *ahimsa* ("harmlessness") in the midst of bloodshed, to talk of God and then kill His creatures. It brings to mind the idea of "holy wars," fought as much for material reasons as for spiritual ones. Thus, I will devote the next chapter to the *Gita*'s setting on a battlefield and its related implications of violence. I can then proceed with my analyses of the *Gita* and *Bagger Vance* in the light of the *Gita*'s three overarching subjects (*karma, jnana,* and *bhakti*).

Violence on the Battlefield of Life

> Make no mistake about it: Golf, the most popular outdoor sport in the U.S., is war.
>
> —B. W. Ollstein, *Combat Golf*

*T*he battles that take place on a golf course are insignificant when compared to those caused by religion. When we contemplate the Crusades, the Inquisition, or, in a more contemporary setting, Waco, Bosnia, Heaven's Gate, the Catholics and the Protestants in Northern Ireland, the Om Shinrikyo attacks in Japan, the bombing of American embassies in Africa, the constant battling between Hindus and Muslims—it makes one think twice about "believers" and their chosen path. How is it that the world's religious traditions, which are supposed to represent spiritual ideals such as love, peace, and mutual understanding, often seem to be instigators of hate and strife? The question is nicely phrased—and, to a degree, answered—by psychotherapist Russell Shorto in his book *Saints and Madmen: Psychiatry Opens Its Doors to Religion:*

> Is it possible that religious feeling—the feeling of oneness with others, of being swept up in the current of cosmic love and eternal goodness—has an element of violence in it? Of

course it does. It is an avenue of human expression, and so will carry whatever baggage people choose to take with them as they travel down it. In the end, the "religion leads to violence" argument falters; you might just as easily say that education leads to violence since there is so much violence in schools. One might counter the argument by borrowing a slogan from the National Rifle Association: Religion doesn't kill, people do. (p. 42)

While I do not necessarily endorse this view when applied to the National Rifle Association, Shorto's point is well taken. Essential religious truths do not promote violence. Rather, people already predisposed to violence interpret these truths in their own distinct way.

Accordingly, a brief look at religious history reveals both martial and peace-loving angles on religion. There are Zionists who are willing to fight for the state of Israel, and there are those like Rabbi Abraham Isaac Kook, who took nonviolence to the point of vegetarianism. The same Islamic tradition that promotes Jihad, or holy war, also gave rise to Abdul Ghaffar Khan, a renowned pacifist. The very existence of someone like Oliver Cromwell, who through military means labored to make England a Christian nation, would lead one to believe that Christianity is a religion that favors violence; but peace advocate George Fox, founder of the Quakers in England and North America, would lead one to believe otherwise. Religion has brought forth the Prince of Peace, Jesus, and personalities such as Gandhi and Mother Teresa. It is also true that most "religious" wars have been fought as much for political and economic reasons as for spiritual ones. Therefore, it seems reasonable to evaluate a given religion on its own spiritual merits, not on the basis of those who have used it to endorse war or violence.

———————— **The Spiritual Warrior** ————————

Few will identify a golf course with a battlefield. Still, like most sports, golf is highly competitive. The difference is that, in golf, you are your own opponent. Bagger Vance elaborates:

> In other sports the opponent is regarded as the enemy. We seek by our actions to disable him. In tennis our stroke defeats him; in football our tackle lays him low. This is not the way to salvation, or, more accurately, it is at one remove. The golfer, on the other hand, is never directly affected by his opponent's actions. He comes to realize that the game is not against his foe, but against himself. His little self. That yammering, fearful, ever-resistant self that freezes, chokes, tops, nobbles, shanks, skulls, duffs, flubs. This is the self we must defeat. (p. 121)

In the *Gita,* too, we learn that our real opponent is our own lower self. We must conquer this self, the *Gita* tells us, with all the attributes afforded us by our higher nature. In other words, we must overcome our conditioning by gaining mastery over our mind and senses. Only then will we be able to see beyond the illusions of material existence and penetrate the higher reality of *bhakti.* As the *Gita* says, "One must liberate himself with the help of his mind—not degrade himself. The mind is the friend of the conditioned soul, but it can be his enemy as well. For the person who has conquered the mind, it is the best of friends. But for one who has failed to do so, it will remain the greatest enemy." (6.5–6)

Conquering the lower self involves adopting the posture of a warrior, spiritually speaking, of course. The *Gita* teaches that there are essentially four highly capable soldiers on the opposing army, and that they must be defeated: In addition to the mind, there are the temptations of the tongue, belly, and genitals. A person on the spiritual path must be serious about the battle, conquering these foes, who so often distract us from spiritual life. Once these adversaries defect, or come to our side, they become our most noble warriors, our most dependable assets.

It should be remembered that R. Junah, according to Pressfield's novel, was a guilt-ridden war hero, who eventually lost his life in the Second World War. Arjuna was also a highly regarded soldier, if considerably more successful. In fact, the narrator of the *Bagger Vance* story seems to indicate that Junah is a more current incarnation of Arjuna, and that the golf field of 1931 was, on a subtle plane, a modern-day refiguring of Arjuna's battlefield:

> I heard voices, skyborne and titanic, and when I looked, the field had been transformed.
>
> It was the battle.
>
> The battle of twenty-one thousand years ago.
>
> That turf which had been fairway a moment past was now torn and sundered by the hoof-strikes of warhorses, the tread of armored infantry digging for traction, the pounding wheels and axles of monstrous engines of war. Rain and blood mingled in the chewed-up muck as steel-girded phalanxes surged past and the clamor of shield upon shield thundered heavenward into the storm.
>
> I saw Junah, valorous as a god, not his present self but some brilliant primordial incarnation, slashing forward aboard a war chariot. (pp. 180–81)

It should not be surprising that, on some level, Junah and Arjuna are the same person. The metaphor of spiritual seeker as warrior is a common one, and for good reason. The spiritual pursuit is like a battle. Our material body, mind, and senses are immediate—they are in our face. The spiritual side of life needs to be nurtured, to be uncovered. For most of us, it is far less immediate and can even be something of a struggle. To set aside the material in favor of the spiritual, then, is, in a sense, like swimming against the waves. According to the *Gita,* we have two choices: to float along with the material conception of life, or to swim upstream to spiritual enlightenment.

Arjuna Gets into the Swing of Things

Arjuna was quite literally a soldier. He was part of the ancient Varnashrama society, which is mentioned in the *Gita* (4.13) as a natural social system emphasizing quality (*guna*) and work (*karma*). The Gita explains that this system takes into account each person's individual nature, and this separates it from most other forms of social stratification.

The Varnashrama system is comprised of four groups, (1) priest and intellectuals, (2) political and military leaders, (3) farmers and merchants, and (4) the proletariat, including artisans—four natural social divisions found in one form or another in any given society. In India, these four are known as *brahmana, kshatriya, vaishya,* and *shudra,* respectively. A similar social structure is mentioned by Plato in the *Republic,* though slaves take the place of *shudras.* Many scholars say that the similarity is too great to be accidental—the connection, it is often thought, must have come through the Pythagoreans, whose teachings have much in common with that of ancient India.

The "quality and work" components sharply distinguish Varnashrama from the much later caste system, which divides society according to one's birth. Using birth as a sole criterion for class distinction causes problems. The son of a priest or an intellectual, for example, is not necessarily inclined to the same kind of work as his father. Or, to give another example, imagine a talented artist trying to convince her daughter that she was born to paint, even though, despite all endeavor, the little girl is unable to draw a straight line. The point is straightforward: Simply because one is born into a particular family does not mean that one will adopt the qualitative traits of his or her parents.

However, everyone does have some natural inclination (either from birth or later acquired) and should certainly be engaged in their respective field. This is Varnashrama. When one engages one's unique, special, God-given propensity, it is believed, one is that much closer to finding one's Authentic Swing. Or, to quote Bagger Vance:

> "I believe that each of us possesses, inside ourselves," Bagger Vance began, "one true Authentic Swing that is ours alone. It is folly to try to teach us another, or mold us to some ideal version of the perfect swing. Each player possesses only that one swing that he was born with, that swing which existed within him before he ever picked up a club. Like the statue of David, our Authentic Swing already exists, concealed within the stone, so to speak." (p. 68)

When Vance says that we each possess our own true nature and that it is "folly to try to teach us another," Krishna concurs. In two places in the *Gita,* Krishna says, "It is far better to perform duties consistent with one's nature, even though such duties may be faulty, than to perform

VIOLENCE ON THE BATTLEFIELD OF LIFE

another's duties" (3.35). And again, "It is better to engage in one's own natural work, even though one may perform it imperfectly, than to accept another's work and perform it perfectly" (18.47).

Acting within the Varnashrama system, Arjuna was a *kshatriya* (an administrative officer), and to execute this properly was his Authentic Swing. In order to understand his plight, we would need to understand something of the *kshatriyas'* duty and the codes by which they lived. The etymology of the word is itself revealing: *kshat* means "hurt." And *trayate* means "to give protection." One who protects from harm or violence, then, is called *kshatriya.*

So a *kshatriya* is a defender, a protector. He is not *violent,* but, rather, he *protects* from violence. There will always be violence in this world, and so there must always be protectors of the innocent. To this end, a *kshatriya* is trained in the military arts. He is noble and chivalrous. But, if necessary, he will employ combative tactics. Because there are people who perform evil deeds, *kshatriyas* such as Arjuna are needed.

In a sense, we are all *kshatriyas*—spiritual warriors, as stated earlier. Whether one is playing an eighteen-hole round of golf, poring through the *Gita's* eighteen chapters, or literally standing on a battlefield—there is a real-life skirmish that must be fought and won. But we must fight on God's behalf. As Vance says, "Therefore, Junah, rest in me. Enter the Field like a warrior. Purged of ego, firm in discipline, seeking no reward save the stroke itself. Give the shot to me" (p. 186).

Whether we think the battle is on Krewe Island, where Bagger Vance speaks his truth, or in the land of the Kurus (also known as Kurukshetra), where Krishna speaks His— for each of us, there is war raging within.

In the first verse of the *Gita*, Kurukshetra (the battlefield) is referred to as Dharmakshetra, the field of *dharma*, of duty and righteousness. The implication is that the *Gita*'s teaching transcends its battlefield surroundings. The conflict portrayed in the *Gita* involves eternal rivals: justice and injustice, good and evil, reality and illusion, matter and spirit. Bagger Vance informs R. Junah that the golf field, too, properly conceived, is more than just a golf field: It is Dharmakshetra.

Mahabharata
The Ultimate Playing Field

Indian sages have carefully preserved the details of the civil war that took place at Kurukshetra (a vast land area that still exists today, about eighty-five miles north of modern Delhi). The entire story is preserved in the *Mahabharata,* which Guinness calls "the longest poem ever written"—over 110,000 couplets. The *Bhagavad-gita* is embedded in this epic poem and is arguably its most popular section. Unlike *The Legend of Bagger Vance,* both *Mahabharata* and *Bhagavad-gita* are believed to be historical fact.

While the date of the *Mahabharata* war is debated among Western scholars, tradition says it occurred five thousand years ago and that the great sage Vyasadeva put the *Gita* and the rest of the *Mahabharata* into written form at that time.

The main focus of the *Mahabharata* involves courtly intrigue, all centering on an important political family of the time. This family consisted of the Kauravas and the Pandavas, two groups of feuding cousins. King Dhritarashtra, the father of the Kauravas, was congenitally blind. Thus, the throne that would have been his, was instead given to his younger brother Pandu, father of the Pandavas.

Dhritarashtra resented Pandu for this and never forgave him. After Pandu's early death, Dhritarashtra received at his court Pandu's five sons—Yudhishthira, Arjuna, Bhima, Nakula, and Sahadeva (the Pandavas)—and, out of duty, raised them with his own children.

Even when the Kauravas and the Pandavas were young boys, rivalry developed between them. The Kauravas were devious and the Pandavas virtuous. As they grew older, the Kauravas used their military might for selfish purposes, while the Pandavas were greatly loved and spiritual-minded political leaders. Still, Dhritarashtra naturally favored his own boys, even though it was clear that the Pandavas were better suited to rule the kingdom.

The sons of Pandu were eventually given territory of their own, where they erected a great city. However, Duryodhana, the eldest son of Dhritarashtra and leader of the Kauravas, was jealous and plotted to take the territory of the Pandavas by dubious means. He "arranged" a game—not golf, but it might as well have been—in which the eldest son of Pandu, Yudhishthira, was sure to lose. The plot succeeded, Yudhishthira lost his kingdom, and the Pandavas were sent into exile for thirteen years.

As true *kshatriyas* of their day, the Pandavas honored their (albeit rigged) defeat and entered the forest for the allotted time of their prescribed exile. Their understanding was that they would regain their kingdom when the exile came to an end. However, after the thirteen years, Duryodhana still denied them the kingdom that was rightfully theirs. They then asked for five small villages, because, as *kshatriyas*, it was their inclination and duty to rule.

Duryodhana, however, was cruel. He denied them any consideration, boasting that they "would not be able to stick a pin into the amount of land that he would give them." Thus, by his humiliating response and his refusal to grant them even small villages, he instigated what was to become a devastating battle.

Although peace was preferred by the Pandavas—and the *Mahabharata* makes careful record of this—war was unavoidable.

Lord Krishna, known by the cousins as God incarnate, was acting as the leader of the Yadavas from Dwaraka, a magnificent city on India's western coast. He offered Himself and His entire army to the cause of the upcoming battle. But both parties would have to choose one or the other. Krishna stipulated that He would do no battle—the side that chose Him would have to be content with his moral support. He would also act as a charioteer. The opposing side would have His nearly endless group of warriors, all highly trained.

Materialistic Duryodhana quickly chose the armed battalions. The righteous Pandavas, on the other hand, asked for Krishna alone, confident that God's grace is more significant than all material facility. Krishna, the *Mahabharata* tells us, in letting the two sides choose Him or His army, shows that God is unbiased; if one turns to Him, to whatever degree, He reciprocates accordingly.

Thus, with Krishna as Arjuna's charioteer, the *Bhagavadgita* begins. Both armies are arrayed and ready for combat. But before the war actually begins, Krishna pulls Arjuna's chariot into the middle of the battlefield, where the fabled bowman can see that on both sides there are friends, relatives, and countrymen. Arjuna becomes paralyzed with fear. He has second thoughts about committing to the massive war that lay ahead, in which no one can really win. And Krishna begins to speak, or, rather, to sing.

Bhagavad-gita: An Overview

Gita means "song," and *Bhagavad* refers to "God, the possessor (*vat*) of all opulence (*bhaga*)." *Bhagavad-gita,* therefore, is "the Song of the All-Opulent One"—it embodies the teachings of Bhagavan Lord Krishna (and, some would say, those of Bagger Vance as well).

As we said earlier, the work comes to us in the form of dialogue between Lord Sri Krishna and the princely warrior Arjuna, which occurs just before the onset of the devastating *Mahabharata* war.

Arjuna, putting aside his duty as a *kshatriya,* decides, for personally motivated reasons (his kinsmen and teachers are in the opposing army), not to fight.

Krishna eloquently reminds Arjuna of his immediate social duty (*varna-dharma*) as a warrior, upon whom people are depending, and more importantly, his religious duty (*sanatan-dharma*), as an eternal spiritual entity in relationship with God. The relevance and universality of Krishna's teachings transcend the immediate historical setting of Arjuna's battlefield dilemma.

The dialogue moves through a series of questions and answers that elucidate metaphysical concepts such as the body/soul (matter/spirit) distinction, the principle of non-attached action, the virtues of discipline (*yoga*) and meditation, the place of knowledge (*jnana*) and devotion (*bhakti*). Krishna teaches that perfection lies not in renunciation of the world, but, rather, in disciplined action (*karma-yoga*), which is to be performed without attachment to results (*karmaphalasanga*).

Krishna shows Arjuna His "Universal Form," which includes all of existence, and then His mystical four-armed Vishnu form and, finally, His original two-armed form. He explains His many manifestations, such as Brahman, Paramatma, and Bhagavan, and ultimately reveals that His personal feature supersedes His impersonal aspects. He explains the three modes of material nature—goodness, passion, and ignorance—showing how an understanding of these three qualities, along with knowledge of divine and demoniac natures, can lead to enlightenment. He explains the different kinds of liberation and the ultimacy of surrendering to Him with a heart of devotion. In all, the *Gita* deals with five subjects in detail: material nature, the cosmic manifestation, time, the living entities (and the implications of their actions), and the nature of God (and devotion to Him).

The concept of *dharma* (literally, "duty") is fundamental to *Bhagavad-gita.* The very first word in the *Gita* is *dharma,* and the last one is *mam* ("my," "mine"). Consequently, tradition maintains that all that is taught in between these two words is "my duty." In other words, the *Gita* contains the duty of Everyman.

While many scholars agree that "duty" is an acceptable translation of the Sanskrit *dharma,* the word is difficult to translate. It is used to refer to "religion," "ordinary religiosity," "sacred duty," "virtue," "cosmic order," and so on. Etymologically, it derives from the verbal root *dhr*, which means "to hold," giving the sense of "that which holds everything together." Things are held together by their essential qualities. *Dharma* is consequently seen as "a given thing's essence," or "a thing's inherent nature." The *dharma* of water is wetness. The *dharma* of honey is sweetness. And, according to Vaishnavas, the *dharma* of the soul is service to Krishna in love and devotion.

In Julius Lipner's recent book on the *Gita* entitled *The Fruits of Desiring: An Enquiry into the Ethics of the Bhagavad-gita for Our Times,* there is an insightful essay by Jacqueline Hirst, lecturer in comparative religion at the University of Manchester. Her essay, entitled "Upholding the World: *Dharma* in the *Bhagavad-gita*," includes a wonderful summary of the *Gita* with special attention to the concept of *dharma* (p. 48):

> On the face of it, the issue of *dharma* in the *Bhagavadgita* is remarkably simple. Arjuna faces a moral dilemma, a pair of "dharmic pulls" between clan duty (*kula-dharma*) and warrior duty (*kshatriya-dharma*), in which following the latter seems to involve destroying the former and with it the whole social fabric (1.28–46). Krishna gives him a new context in which to assess his apparent dilemma (the self does not really slay nor is it slain, 2.19f., so act with detachment, 2.47), and a quite straightforward teaching: it is better to perform your own *dharma* imperfectly than another's well (3.35). The dilemma is dissolved. A clear course of action emerges (and is, indeed, followed). End of story, since the recommendation is reiterated in ch. 18 (especially 18.43–48).

What Exactly Do We Mean by Violence?

Ironically, the *Mahabharata* ultimately teaches the opposite of violence: *ahimsa paro dharmo*, "Harmlessness is the greatest duty." The *Gita* itself praises harmlessness (*ahimsa*) throughout its pages. In 10.4–5, *ahimsa* is glorified as a quality created directly by Krishna; in 13.8–12, it is described as knowledge as opposed to ignorance; in 16.2–3 it is a characteristic of divine nature, as opposed to the demoniac; and in 17.14 it is lauded as a desirable austerity of the body. Therefore, to reject the *Bhagavad-gita* because of blatant violence is unacceptable; the *Gita* itself rejects violence.

In general, the word *violence* refers to an overt physical act of destruction: someone is manhandled, pushed, hit, stabbed, raped, or in some other way made the object of physical abuse. This definition is reinforced by most dictionaries. The initial definition in *Webster's Collegiate Dictionary* (fifth edition) describes *violence* as the "exertion of any physical force considered with reference to its effect on another than the agent." The initial definition of the adjective *violent* is similar: "moving, acting, or characterized by physical force, especially by extreme and sudden or by unjust or improper force."

According to the Eisenhower Commission, which some years ago conducted research on violence in America, something is violent when it is seen "to inflict physical injury to people or damage to property." Another conventional definition, found in George Edwards's book *Jesus and the Politics of Violence,* is this: "Violence is physical force resulting in injury or destruction of property or persons in violation of general moral belief or civil law."

These descriptions of violence are tangible and direct; of course, the *Bhagavad-gita* itself is simply devoid of this kind of violence.

But Krishna does encourage Arjuna to engage in battle—and a battle does indeed take place later in the *Mahabharata*. Gandhi, well known for his pacifism, was concerned about this. Still, even *he* acknowledged that righteous battle has a proper time and place, that violence can sometimes be engaged in for a higher good. This is clear in *Mohandas Gandhi: The Man and His Vision:* "I have come to see," wrote Gandhi, "what I did not so clearly before, that there is sometimes nonviolence in violence. . . . I had not fully realized the duty of restraining a drunkard from doing evil, or killing a dog in agony or one infected with rabies. In all such instances, violence is in fact nonviolence" (p. 10).

Along similar lines, Indian historian S. Dasgupta is quoted in *Mohandas Gandhi* as asking and answering the following question: If a dangerous beast enters a cattle shed, should one kill the beast or let it destroy the valuable cattle? Kill the beast, he concludes, for the principal objective is to maintain social order and the well-being of the people (p. 15). According to the *Gita,* this principle supersedes any abstraction, such as unqualified nonviolence (which is often an extremist position), that may result in more harm done than good.

Nonviolence, of course, is a quality cherished by many—and especially by those who follow the *Bhagavad-gita*—but it must be approached with practicality. Total nonviolence may be a diplomatic ideal, but it is never fully realized: Even when we breathe, we unintentionally kill tens of thousands of microorganisms. As long as breathing is a part of life, such "violence" is unavoidable.

It is clear from the *Gita* that if Arjuna did not engage in battle, the demoniac forces of the opposing army would overburden the world with degradation and destruction. It was thus Arjuna's duty to fight, since fighting in this case would be the lesser of two evils.

In Summary
Hit the Ball Where It Lies

In an essay entitled "The Gita and War," which is appended to their translation of the *Gita*, Swami Prabhavananda and Christopher Isherwood thoroughly analyze Arjuna's dilemma as a prince of peace who finds himself in an arena of battle. Much of what follows in this chapter is a sort of paraphrased summary of their writing. They begin by asserting that to understand the *Gita*, one must first consider what it is and what it is not. Krishna and Arjuna are on a battlefield—they are *not* on a golf course. Neither is Arjuna a renunciant. He is a warrior. His problem should be considered in relation to his particular circumstances; he must decide what to do while on a battlefield.

In teaching Arjuna, Krishna adopts two approaches: the relative and the absolute. He begins by dealing with Arjuna's feeling of trepidation. Arjuna, for his part, is too frightened to think clearly, and so the last thing he wants is participation in the war—even though it is his duty to protect the righteous. Krishna first reminds him that the soul is eternal and can never truly be slain. He explains that bodily existence is not what it seems to be—birth and death are illusory in that they are temporary. Only that which lasts, Krishna says, can be considered real in the truest sense. Having explained this in a detailed and comprehensive manner, Krishna goes on to discuss Arjuna's individual problem.

For Arjuna, as a noble warrior meant to give protection to the people, the fighting of this battle is unquestionably righteous. His cause is just, and to defend it is his duty. Everyone, explains Krishna, can attain the highest level of consciousness by following the prescribed path of his own natural duty while being conscious of God. Religion is simply the science of learning how to do this. Throughout the world and throughout the pages of history, there have been those who have reached spiritual perfection while carrying out their duties as merchants, peasants, doctors, popes, kings, and golf pros. It is not so much what you do, says the *Gita*, as whom you do it for.

Prabhavananda and Isherwood remind us that in the purely physical sense of action, Arjuna is, indeed, no longer a free agent. The act of war is upon him; and he must do his duty. We are meant to learn from this. At any given moment, we must hit the ball where it lies. We cannot arbitrarily pretend to be in a different situation. In other words, we must deal with our circumstances. The *Gita* teaches the art of doing this while being conscious of God. Only through this acceptance of our given situation can we begin to evolve further. We may select the battleground, say Prabhavananda and Isherwood, but we cannot avoid the battle.

Arjuna is bound to act, but he is free to choose exactly *how* he will perform the action. In general, one acts with attachment—we want a particular result. This, of course, means that we act with materially motivated desire. And fear. We have desire for a certain result and we have fear that this result will not be obtained. Such attached action, the *Gita* teaches, binds us to the world of action and reaction—to the continual doing of more materially motivated action.

But there is another way of performing action, one that transcends fear or personal desire—performing action on behalf of God. This is the *Gita*'s central teaching. Prabhavananda and Isherwood point out that Christians refer to such detached action as "holy indifference" and that Hindus call it "nonattachment." Both terms are slightly misleading, they say, for these terms suggest coldness and a lack of enthusiasm. That is why people often confuse nonattachment with fatalism, when, actually, they are opposites. The fatalist simply does not care. He knows his fate is unavoidable, and for this reason he decides not to make any effort.

But the doer of real nonattached action, as described in the *Gita,* is the most conscientious of people. Freed from fear and materially motivated desire, such a person offers everything he does as a sacrament of devotion to the Lord. All work becomes equally important—imbued with new meaning. It is only toward the fruits of work, or, more specifically, the fruitive mentality—with its concomitant dualities of success or failure, praise or blame—that he remains indifferent. When action is done in this spirit, Krishna teaches, it gradually leads to the realization of what is behind action, behind all life: the Supreme Lord and one's relationship with Him.

Thus, the *Gita* teaches a hybrid philosophy of fate and human effort, determinism and free will. As the late R. C.

Zaehner, *Gita* commentator and well-known teacher of Hinduism, Sanskrit, and Indian studies, has explained it in his book simply titled *Hinduism:*

> Though the *Mahabharata* stresses time and again the primacy of fate over human effort, it nonetheless compares the two to the rain which prepares the ground and the seed that man puts into it (5.78.2–5): the two are interdependent and work in harmony together. Human *karma* is but a fraction of the *karma* of the whole universe, and this totality of *karma* adds up to fate, and fate itself is under the control of God. Fate is the cosmic *dharma* from which man cannot escape; and in the long run it is man's co-operation with fate which is but another word for God's will that justifies him and earns him a place in heaven. (pp. 106–7)

In fact, then, the *Gita* presents a balanced view of reality, harmonizing philosophical opposites in a coherent, workable manner. Apropos of this, it neither sanctions war nor condemns it. Nor is it about peace as opposed to violence. Rather, the *Gita* is about action versus inaction. It happens to take place on a battlefield, but it could have transpired anywhere—even on a golf course.

The golfer should golf. The painter should paint. The musician should make music. And the warrior should fight. The *Gita* is about doing what you do with a spiritual end in mind—but do it you must. The secret, of course, is to recognize yourself as an instrument, to recognize God as the ultimate "Doer" behind each act. It is the acquisition of this mind-set that the *Gita* bequeaths to its readers.

The pacifist must respect the righteous warrior, and the warrior, the pacifist—*if* they are both acting on God's behalf. The spiritual warrior and the spiritual pacifist are going toward the same goal, spiritual realization. There is an underlying solidarity between them, culminating in that consciousness of God which transcends all duality—culminating in Krishna consciousness.

We conclude with the words of one of the twentieth century's best-known pacifists, Thomas Merton, who writes in his essay "The Significance of the Bhagavad-gita":

> The *Gita* is not a justification of war, nor does it propound a war-making mystique. . . . Arjuna has an instinctive repugnance for war, and that is the chief reason why war is chosen as the example of the most repellant kind of duty. The *Gita* is saying that even in what appears to be most "unspiritual" one can act with pure intentions and thus be guided by Krishna consciousness. This consciousness itself will impose the most strict limitations on one's use of violence because that use will not be directed by one's own selfish interests, still less by cruelty, sadism, and mere blood lust. (p. 20)

3

The Art of Action

All men are forced to act by an impulse born of material
nature. Therefore, no one can refrain from doing something, not even for a moment.

—*Bhagavad-gita* 3.5

Life *is* action, Junah. Even choosing not to act, we act. We
cannot do otherwise. Therefore, act with vigor!

—Bagger Vance, 98

*T*he first six chapters of the *Gita* focus on *karma*
(action). The second six on *bhakti* (devotion).
And the final six on *jnana* (knowledge). I will here
take the reader through the *Gita* in this order, even though
tradition ascribes a more important place to *bhakti* (and so
one would expect it to come last). Interestingly, the disciplic
lineages have compared the *Gita* to "a sandwich" in which
the most important part is found in the middle. In other
words, *bhakti* is "sandwiched" in between *karma* and *jnana*.
According to Prabhupada, "The first six and the last six
chapters are like coverings for the middle six chapters,
which are especially protected by the Lord. If one is fortunate enough to understand *Bhagavad-gita*—especially these
middle six chapters—in the association of devotees, then his

life at once becomes glorified beyond all penances, sacrifices, charities, speculations, etc., for one can achieve all the results of these activities simply by Krishna consciousness" (8.28, *Bhagavad-gita As It Is,* purport).

There are those who say that *jnana* is superior to *bhakti,* and they use as evidence the fact that the *Gita* treats *jnana* as its final consideration. However, the tradition is clear that *jnana* is subservient to *bhakti.* William Deadwyler, in his essay entitled "The Contribution of Bhagavata-Dharma Toward a 'Scientific Religion' and a 'Religious Science,'" explains why *bhakti* is supreme (pp. 366–81):

> The *Bhagavad-gita* recognizes that the natural spiritual development from *karma* to *jnana* to *bhakti* is very slow and very difficult. There are many ways to become baffled and deviated from the course. Thus, Krishna states that only after undergoing the trouble of many births does one who is actually wise—i.e., developed in *jnana*—surrender unto Him, saying "Vasudeva [Krishna] is everything." Such a great soul, Krishna says, is very rare. (Bg. 7.19)

The point here is that after rigorous karmic and yogic pursuits, one may develop true knowledge (*jnana*). Having accomplished this, a few rare souls actually have enough *jnana* to surrender to Krishna with love and devotion. Thus *bhakti* is the perfection of *jnana,* and not the other way around.

Deadwyler elaborates on this point:

> . . . *jnana* is not the ultimate, but the penultimate, stage of spiritual development. According to the *Bhagavad-gita,* if *jnana* is properly cultivated to maturity, it undergoes a further transformation into *bhakti* (7.9). . . . The stage of *jnana* is not yet complete knowledge. It is a reactionary stage, anti-

thetical to *karma,* and therefore bound to it, as the negation of a proposition is bound to the proposition. It seeks the absolute through negation of relative names, forms, qualities, and so on, yet these negations, being opposites, are themselves therefore relative, and as such, fall short of disclosing the absolute. In both thought and action, *jnana* rejects the world of objects, names, senses, desires, and activities.

Deadwyler takes these thoughts to their natural conclusion:

If, for example, the thesis is "form" (*karma*), then the antithesis (*jnana*) is "formless." How do we overcome this duality, this opposition? What do we seek that is form and formless at the same time? The resolution is disclosed on the platform of *bhakti.* At this stage knowledge of the Absolute attains completion—and beyond the undifferentiated light there is revealed within transcendence a supreme entity of spiritual variegatedness, the manifest absolute truth, the Personality of Godhead. This disclosure of transcendental, or spiritual, form unites the opposition of form and formless: there is form but no form, i.e., no material form. . . . Neither *karma* nor *jnana* have access to transcendental form, for neither the perceptions of the material senses [as in *karma*] nor the negation of them [as in *jnana*] can apprehend it. But when, in relationship with the Supreme Person, spiritual senses are manifest by acting in devotion, transcendental form becomes cognizable. . . . *Bhakti* sublates both *karma* and *jnana,* fusing action and inaction, form and formlessness. The world, denied in *jnana,* returns in *bhakti,* but in a wholly transfigured manner; it is not the profane world enjoyed or renounced by the *karmi* or the *jnani.* In both cases, the world is unrelated to the Supreme, but the *bhakta* sees the world as intrinsically related, as energy to the energetic source, as one with God yet different from Him at the same time. God and God's energies constitute a whole absolute truth, a unity that includes, not excludes, diversity.

All of this will have more meaning as we analyze the *Gita* in relation to *karma, bhakti,* and *jnana.*

Arjuna Gets Teed Off

As the *Gita* opens, Arjuna is confronted with an existential dilemma. He has to deeply consider his identity, his purpose in life. He is faced with many of the same questions that eventually come to us all. Who am I? What should I be doing? What is more important: occupation or family and friends?

In Arjuna's case, the questions are all the more poignant for being asked on a battlefield, where life or death results from the answers. In the midst of the emotional turmoil, he tells Krishna his initial decision: "Govinda [an intimate name for Krishna], I shall not fight" (2.9). Still, seeing his family and friends on the opposing side, as stated earlier, he is teed off.

The parallel section in *Bagger Vance* is equally dramatic, as I have shown in the introduction. After much haranguing, Junah, like his *Bhagavad-gita* counterpart, bluntly proclaims, "I won't play" (p. 27).

The philosophical teachings of the *Gita* begin in the second chapter. Confused about what he must do—the proper course of action—Arjuna situates himself as Krishna's disciple and asks for instruction: "Now I am confused about duty and have lost all sense due to weakness. In this condition I am asking You to tell me what is best for me. I state it now directly: I am Your disciple—a soul surrendered unto You. Please tell me what to do" (2.7).

Junah similarly submits to Vance: "Do you think I want to feel these awful emotions, that I take pleasure in the desperate conclusions my heart leads me to? I'm lost, Bagger. Help me, my friend and mentor. Tell me what I must do" (p. 97). The relationships are similar: Arjuna is Krishna's devotee and friend; Junah is Vance's devotee and friend. This section also shows that both the *Gita* and *Bagger Vance* recommend the principle of submitting to a teacher. Most people today, however, look at the *guru*/disciple relationship with a bit of skepticism.

As author Andrew Vidich writes in *Love Is a Secret: The Mystic Quest for Divine Love:*

> We in the West are often averse to seeing the need for a living spiritual master. Yet in every other field of endeavor, we are hesitant to proceed without a teacher. We would shun a doctor or lawyer who had not taken the appropriate studies at an accredited institution with experts in the field. The refusal, in our culture, to accept a spiritual authority reflects our society's disregard for tradition. (p. 42)

Nonetheless, both Krishna and Bagger Vance teach that a spiritual master is essential for pursuing higher spiritual studies. The *Gita* makes this clear in 4.34 as Vance does by his very presence on the golf course. Pressfield expressed the guru concept nicely in a recent interview:

> I think we all at some level respond to the idea of a personal mentor, call him God, Guru, Messiah, Savior. It's like putting a human face on the great mystery. We want a buddy we can turn to, who knows more than we do, who can instruct us and guide us when we've lost our way.

Once Arjuna submits himself as a disciple, Krishna adopts the role of a teacher. He begins instructing Arjuna by telling him that he is foolish. But He says it in the nicest way:

> While speaking in an intelligent way, you are mourning for that which is not worthy of grief. The wise do not lament for the living or the dead. (2.11)

This scene is approximated in *Bagger Vance*:

> Junah's eyes rose now and met Bagger Vance's. "I have been a warrior," he said in a voice tremulous with emotion. "I have fought, and nearly died, in battles as grave and calamitous as any in the history of man. I have seen friends perish, and enemies who might have been friends but for the madness of war. I will never take up arms again"—he gestured toward the bag and its clubs—"even surrogates as preposterous as these."
>
> Saying this, Junah slumped yet deeper onto the running board, his mind tormented by grief.
>
> Now Bagger Vance spoke. "This conduct is disgraceful," he said. "Unworthy of any man, but more so of you, Rannulph Junah, whom I hold dear and bless beyond all others. Get ahold of yourself! It provokes me to fury, to see you cast down your eyes and give voice to such ignoble thoughts!" (p. 96)

—— The Song of the Perfect Caddie-Master ——

Bhagavan Sri Krishna begins to enlighten Arjuna by presenting what is known in India as Sankhya—the analytical study of matter and spirit (2.11–30). To alleviate Arjuna's distress (at the thought of killing his friends and relatives), Krishna contrasts the eternality of the soul (the real self) with the temporary nature of the material body (the soul's outer covering). The soul, Krishna teaches, is eternal. It continues to exist after the death of the body: "For the soul there is no such thing as birth or death. And having once existed, he never ceases to be. He is unborn, eternal, ever-existing, undying, and primeval. He does not die when the body is finished" (2.20). Krishna further explains that, at death, the soul transmigrates to a new body: "As a person puts on new clothes, putting aside those garments that are old and worn, similarly, the soul accepts new material bodies, giving up the old and useless ones" (2.22). Or, further still, "As the embodied soul continuously incarnates, in this one lifetime, from childhood to youth to old age, the soul similarly takes on another body at death" (2.13). The wise man is he who, knowing the self to be the eternal soul (and not the body), is never disturbed by the change of his outer dress ("death") and is unconcerned with its temporary pleasures and pains. Such a person, Krishna says, is eligible for liberation from material embodiment.

Krishna is here referring to the soul and reincarnation. For many of us, belief in such things requires a leap of faith. Not so for Arjuna or the culture in which he lived. The non-material essence that makes a living being "alive" and the principle of reincarnation—that the living being travels to a new body when its present one can no longer accommodate it—were as central to Vedic culture as paying taxes is to most of us.

Modern science also recognizes a sort of spark, or energy, that animates the body, something that distinguishes it from dead matter. Further, the first law of thermodynamics, stating that energy cannot be created or destroyed, gives us reason to pause when thinking about reincarnation—if there is energy in the body, and this energy cannot be created or destroyed, where does it go at the time of death?

When Krishna likens reincarnation to the changing of garments (2.22, above), or to the many bodies—childhood, youth, old age—that we experience in this one lifetime (2.13, above), He is offering rather vivid analogies. The *Gita* is essentially saying that there is a hint of reincarnation in day-to-day life. Science has shown that, if one lives a seventy-year life, he has gone through virtually ten different bodies. This is because cells are constantly replicating themselves, so that by the time approximately seven years is up, every cell in the body has been replaced with a new one. Thus, in this very lifetime, we are reborn a number of times. The *Gita* suggests that this process does not stop with death, but rather that we continue to change into a still newer body. This view of reincarnation is not peculiar to the *Gita.* Most Hindu-based texts, known as the Vedic literature, endorse the view that the soul travels from one body to another at the time of death, and that we can see a hint of it in the many bodies we take on in this one lifetime. This conception of going from one body to another is called in Sanskrit *samsara,* or the cycle of birth and death.

Along these same lines, Vedic texts express a dissatisfaction with the linear view of reality, saying that such a view defies what we experience in nature. Rather, the Vedic tradition endorses a cyclical view of existence. Vaishnava sages bring to our attention that the sun does not simply rise and set; it does so repeatedly. The seasons recur, one after the other; huge ages, or *yugas*, also exist in cycles. Even the hands on a watch or clock do not stop after a full day has passed—they go on and on. In this way, Vaishnava sages tell us, the living being does not die with the body but incarnates again and again.

Believe it or not, much has been made of the link between golf and reincarnation. The connection probably begins with an old Scottish golf saying, "The game was invented a billion years ago—don't you remember?" Michael Murphy, author of *Golf in the Kingdom,* indicates that golf is itself suggestive of the cyclical nature of reality:

> And—you might have guessed it—a round of golf is good for that, ". . . because if it is a journey, it is also a *round:* it always leads back to the place you started from . . . golf is always a trip back to the first tee, the more you play, the more you realize you are staying where you are." By playing golf, he said, "you reenact that secret of the journey. You may even get to enjoy it." (p. 134)

Come Again?

For most of us, these ideas are somewhat foreign. However, if these same ideas are expressed in familiar terms, they start to become plausible. Take, for example, the Law of Karma, which, as we will soon see, is intimately linked to both the soul and reincarnation. In the East, *karma* is understood as the actions we perform and their inevitable results. A similar principle in the West is Newton's Third Law of Motion: for every action, there is an equal and opposite reaction. Author Mark Mathew Braunstein eloquently brings the Law of Karma into focus for a Western audience. He writes that *karma* can be described "scientifically as action and reaction, epistemologically as cause and effect, biblically and botanically as sowing and reaping, and even economically as supply and demand" (*Radical Vegetarianism,* 89).

When understood in these terms, the Law of Karma seems less exotic, more concrete. Recent findings augment the view that *karma* just makes sense. For example, the studies of Roger Sperry, a Nobel-Prize-winning brain scientist, indicate that the Western principle of cause and effect needs to be broadened. He is quoted in an interesting article by Drutakarma Dasa entitled "Science, the Bomb, and the *Bhagavad-gita*": "We have to recognize . . . different levels and types of causation, including higher kinds of causal control involving mental and vital forces that material science has always rejected" (p. 28). The Law of Karma would be one example of such a higher law.

Along these lines, Huston Smith, a well-known professor of the history of religions and comparative philosophy, writes in *The World's Religions:*

> Science has alerted the Western world to the importance of causal relationships in the physical world. Every physical event, we are inclined to believe, has its causes, and every cause will have its determinate effects. India extends this concept of universal causation to include man's moral and spiritual life as well" (p. 64)

I will return to the Law of Karma later, since it is discussed again in the *Gita*'s third chapter.

Bagger Vance expresses the idea of karma in his own words, "There can be no cheating in the dimension in which the Self resides. There every action inexorably produces its result, every thought its consequence" (p. 122). Vance also elaborates on the nature of the soul:

We enter onto this material plane, as Wordsworth said, "not in utter nakedness, but trailing clouds of glory do we come from God, who is our home." In other words, already possessing a highly refined and individuated soul. Our job here is to recall that soul and become it. (p. 70)

Or, more cryptically,

"Junah's problem is simple," he said. "He thinks he is Junah."

"What in damnation does that mean?" The Judge's face flushed crimson. "He *is* Junah, you damn twit!"

"I will teach him he is *not* Junah," the caddie answered with his accustomed calm. "Then he will swing Junah's swing." (p. 104)

Identity Handicap

When we look at ourselves analytically, we have to confess that we don't know who we really are. Sure, we have external identity: I'm John Smith; I belong to a particular church; have such-and-such a job; I am married, and I am a basically good person. But these are external designations, as changeable as our favorite shirt or color of choice. Names can be changed, as can one's faith, employment, spouse, or temperament.

The one thing that doesn't change is the essence within, that aspect of each person that is reflected in one's consciousness. Religions of the world tend to refer to this essence as "the soul," but it can be referred to in any number of ways. For those who choose to pursue this subject without common religious jargon, let us refer to this essence, as Vance does, merely as "the self."

The origin and destination of this "self" have been the subject of much of philosophy, literature, and science. Where do we come from? Where are we going? What is the best possible way to spend our time while we're here? These are important questions, relevant to every one of us, whether or not we are interested in religion. Nonetheless, the answers to these questions carry strong theological implications, conjuring up speculations about the afterlife and various unknown phenomena. These ideas, again, are inextricably related to the Law of Karma, or the law of causality. In other words, we get what we do. What goes around, comes around. If we act badly, there is some bad reaction waiting; if we act with goodness, goodness awaits. According to the *Gita,* not all reactions can be confined to one lifetime, which is why the "self" reincarnates, again and again, until it pays all its dues and reaps all its rewards. My book *The Reincarnation Controversy* explores the many religious texts and scientific findings that substantiate this reincarnationist worldview.

Vance alludes to reincarnation throughout his dialogue with Junah. The following is a good example of this, also showing that Vance is more than a mere saint (*rishi*):

> ". . . and you were probably there too. One of the reechies."
>
> "Rishis," Vance corrected me gently. "And no, I was not one of them." He paused. "I taught them."
>
> "Of course. You were the pro! Twenty-one thousand years ago. . . . Or was it twenty-one million? When Krewe Island was called Mu." (p. 140)

Much earlier in the book, Vance vividly describes an incident that occurred thousands of years before his time. When he was questioned as to how he could know and graphically describe an event that took place before his birth, he again affirms the doctrine of reincarnation:

> "I was there," Bagger Vance answered casually, as if it were the most obvious thing in the world.
>
> He looked down at me, to see if I believed him. I felt the power of his eyes, their warmth and even love for me. I was held as if by the sun.
>
> "Junah was with me as well," he smiled, still touching my shoulder. "And do you know what, young Hardy? You were there too." (p. 76)

Golf in the Kingdom often refers to the difference between the soul and the body, and that the soul reincarnates when a person dies. Michael Murphy puts it this way: "the evidence is compelling that we do indeed possess another body, an inner body, a vehicle of consciousness that survives death." He goes on to say:

> Psychologies other than our twentieth-century Western model include these dimensions of human experience, and have included them for thousands of years. It has been helpful for me to remember that. Indian psychology, for example, has much to say about the *sukshma sharira,* the so-called "subtle" or "feeling" body; the Upanishads describe various *koshas* or "soul-sheaths." (pp. 144–45)

These sheaths, or bodies, are mentioned in the *Gita,* but they are explained in greater depth in the Upanishads. The soul, it is said, is covered by five "sheaths," some composed of subtle elements and others of those that are more gross. Our first layer is a "bliss sheath"; after this, there is an "intellectual sheath"; and then a "mental sheath"; a "pranic [life air] sheath"; and, finally, a "physical sheath."

We have many bodies, the Upanishads tell us, our outer material body merely being the most visible.

------------ **The Perfect Caddie-Master** ------------
Continues . . .

Since the real self, beneath the many sheaths, is eternal and never subject to death, Arjuna should not lament discharging his duty: "Considering your specific duty as a *kshatriya,* you should know that there is nothing better for you to do than to fight on religious grounds; there is thus no need for you to hesitate" (2.31).

Krishna is about to elucidate the "art of action," also called "the art of work": Karma-yoga. By acting out of selfless duty to the Supreme (without desire for the fruits of action), one attains liberation from material bondage. At its best, this is called Buddhi-yoga. *Buddhi* means "intelligence," and the culmination of using one's intellect in the service of the Lord is called Buddhi-yoga (2.39–53).

All of this *yoga* terminology can be confusing. The whole subject becomes easier to understand when we realize that these different words actually refer to the same thing: the various *yoga* systems are all preliminary forms of Bhakti-yoga. The differences are mainly in emphasis. It is called Karma-yoga, for example, when, in the practitioner's mind, the first word in the hyphenated compound takes precedence—not just in the physical placement of the word, but conceptually. For instance, in Karma-yoga, one wants to perform work (*karma*) and is attached to a particular kind of work, but he wants to do it for Krishna. In this scenario, *karma* is primary and *yoga* is secondary. But since it is directed to God, it can be called Karma-yoga instead of just *karma.* The same principle can be applied to all other *yoga* systems.

Of all *yogas,* however, Bhakti-yoga is the highest. This is because the first word in the hyphenated compound is *bhakti,* or devotional love. In love, one becomes selfless, and thus, instead of giving a prominent place to one's own desire, one considers the beloved first. Thus, the second part of the compound (*yoga*) becomes prominent—linking with God takes precedence over what *I* want. In fact, the first and second words of the hyphenated compound become one. The devotee wants to love (*bhakti*), but he considers Krishna's desire before his own. This makes Bhakti-yoga the perfection of the *yoga* process.

In other words, Karma-yoga emphasizes "working" for the Supreme; Jnana-yoga emphasizes "focusing one's knowledge" on the Supreme; Dhyana-yoga involves "contemplating" the Supreme; Buddhi-yoga is about directing the "intellect" toward the Supreme; and Bhakti-yoga, the perfection of all *yogas,* occurs when "devotion" is emphasized in relation to the Supreme. The main principle of *yoga,* in whatever form, is to direct your activity toward linking with God.

Arjuna wants to know what a true *yogi* is like, and so he asks Krishna to describe one who is self-realized—one who is situated in detached, transcendental consciousness—giving specific characteristics (2.54). Thus, in the remainder of the second chapter, Krishna brings to light the nature of the *sthita-prajna,* or the person fixed in consciousness of the Supreme. Since such self-realized souls are fully aware of their spiritual identity, they are not interested in material pleasure—or, let us say, they are more interested in spiritual pleasure. For this reason, they naturally control their outward senses. With controlled senses and with mind and intelligence fixed on the Supreme, they are unaffected by material dualities such as pain and pleasure, loss and gain. The *sthita-prajna,* at the time of death, attains the spiritual world.

It is significant that the *Gita* offers specific details about the nature of self-realized souls. Cheaters abound. Arjuna specifically asks about the *sthita-prajna* so one can distinguish real saints from those who only make a show. If one studies this section of the *Gita* closely, one is less likely to be deceived by charlatans in spiritual dress.

In describing the self-realized soul, Krishna also explains how one functions if one is *not* self-realized. He tells us that those who are enamored with materialistic life begin simply by contemplating the objects of the senses. Such contemplation naturally leads to self-interested action and, finally, attachment. This, in turn, gives rise to anger. Why anger? Because everything in the world is temporary, and so we eventually lose the objects of our attachment. Anger, Krishna says, leads to bewilderment, and bewilderment to loss of memory. At this point, intelligence is lost. According to Krishna, intelligence means good memory and fine discretion—both of which fall away when we adopt materialistic life. This vicious cycle puts us in a nonspiritual frame of mind, in which we forget who we are, and what life is really all about. Krishna refers to this as "a material whirlpool" that drags people ever lower; it is a complex downward spiral that begins, as He says in the *Gita,* simply by one's contemplating the objects of the senses (2.61–64). Krishna thus tells Arjuna not to be fooled by sensual stimulation and, instead, to control his senses for a higher purpose.

———— A Work of Art: "The Art of Work" ————

In the *Gita's* third chapter, we find that Arjuna is confused by Krishna's instructions thus far. He understands the distinction between the soul and the body, as well as the idea of reincarnation. He further understands that Krishna is telling him to control his senses and to fix his mind and intelligence on the Supreme (which is Buddhi-yoga). But he feels that this latter instruction runs counter to the performance of action, and it seems clear that Krishna wants him to act. He therefore asks Krishna why He is requesting him to engage in warfare—how can he simultaneously fight and be renounced? (3.1–2). Arjuna's mental image of a spiritualist engaged in Buddhi-yoga is obviously someone who goes off to a secluded place and focuses his intellect on the Supreme. Like most people, Arjuna has difficulty understanding how action that seems material can in fact be spiritual.

Arjuna's confusion is inherited by Junah, who also misunderstands Vance:

> "But all this you know, Junah. I repeat it now only to focus your distracted mind under this excruciating pressure. To return you to the imperative to act."
>
> Here Junah, who had been listening with as much attention as he could muster under the circumstances, bridled and pulled up in midstride. "I don't understand you, Bagger," he said. "You order me to win, as if I could, but in the same breath you tell me to love my opponents. Please be clear. I need to understand what you're telling me."
>
> "Act, Junah, but act without attachment, as the earth does. As I do. The rain falls, with no thought of watering the

land. The clouds roll, not seeking to bring shade. They simply do. And we must too." (pp. 122–23)

In response to Arjuna's confusion, Krishna explains Karma-yoga, the performance of actions free from desire for selfish, fruitive gain, actions that are dedicated to God (3.3–35). This clears up much of Arjuna's doubt. Previously, he had thought that all work is fruitive and leads to bondage, that renunciation was the only truly spiritual path. Krishna explains to him, however, that one can avoid sinful reactions through devotional work, and that this is in fact better than attempting to escape reactions by renouncing the world.

The *Gita* teaches us to do our work. But it first teaches that *karma*, or action, brings either material enjoyment or material suffering, depending on what we do. Whether the results of a given action are pleasant or unpleasant, they bind us to the bondage of repeated birth and death in the material world. Krishna explains that "inaction" is insufficient to save us from material reactions. By nature, everyone is forced to act. Work is fundamental to existence.

As Huston Smith writes in *The World's Religions*:

Work is the staple of human life. The point is not simply that all but a few people must work to survive. Ultimately, the drive to work is psychological rather than economic. Forced to be idle most people become irritable; forced to retire, they decline. . . . To such people [*Bhagavad-gita*] says, You don't have to retire to a cloister to realize God. You can find God in the world of everyday affairs as readily as anywhere. Throw yourself into your work with everything you have; only do so wisely, in a way that will bring the highest rewards, not just trivia. Learn the secret of work by which

every movement can carry you Godward even while other
things are being accomplished, like a wristwatch that winds
itself as other duties are performed. (p. 37)

By this method, says the *Gita,* one can work in such a way
as to avoid further material bondage, leading to ultimate
liberation. That art of work is Karma-yoga—working and
acting under the direction of the Supreme for His satisfaction: "Work done as a sacrifice to God has to be performed.
Otherwise, work binds one to this material world. Therefore, O son of Kunti [Arjuna], perform your natural duties
for His satisfaction, and in that way you will always remain
unattached and free from bondage" (3.9). The *Gita* later
explains that the performance of Karma-yoga gradually ele-
vates one to Bhakti-yoga, or pure devotion for Krishna.

The *Gita* next discusses *yajna* (sacrifice)—duties that are
prescribed in the *Vedas* (3.10–16). One who is fully self-
realized, says the *Gita,* no longer needs to perform such
duties, for he is already purified and thus his duty is directly
enunciated by the Lord. He should continue, however, to
perform duties non-fruitively, to set a good example for
those yet attached to the fruits of work (3.17–29). Having
thoroughly explained both Karma-yoga and *yajna,* Krishna
sums up the essence of His teaching thus far: "Surrendering
all your works unto Me, with mind focused on Me, and
without desire for gain and free from egoism and lethargy—
fight." Then Krishna essentially reiterates the difference
between *karma* and Karma-yoga, explaining that everyone
must act, but if one acts selfishly, without controlling the
senses, one becomes bound to the material world. If one
acts for Krishna, one becomes free and happy in this life.
And meets Krishna in the next (3.30–35).

⸻ Lust: "Out-of-Bounds" for the Soul ⸻

In the last part of the *Gita*'s third chapter, Arjuna asks a very significant question, "What causes a person to act sinfully, even if they are not willing, as if engaged by force?" (3.36). Krishna answers that it is lust (material desire), which He says is the "destroyer of knowledge and self-realization." After locating the problem for Arjuna, He prescribes the method for overcoming it: sense regulation inspired by spiritual knowledge. The senses, mind, and intelligence are the three "sitting places" of lust. Knowing the self to be transcendental to these three, "one should control the lower self by the higher self and thus—by spiritual strength—conquer this insatiable enemy known as lust" (3.37–43).

This is an important teaching. In golf, the area outside the boundaries of the course is called "out-of-bounds." If a ball finishes "O.B.," as it is sometimes called, the player must return to the original spot and play another ball with the penalty of one stroke. This can be quite a setback in one's game. Similarly, Krishna reveals that lust is "out-of-bounds" for the aspiring spiritualist, and that if one submits to lusty desire, one's "game" will suffer greatly.

Vance, it may be remembered, told Junah the importance of conquering the lower self with the higher self. Such conquest is essential if one is to pursue spiritual life, or even just to be happy in the material world. What we are "conquering" here is our own conditioning. Deep-rooted habits are not always easy to overcome. But if one develops a higher taste, it becomes natural to give up a lower one. Life affords many hints of this. A young boy, for example, may love to play with toys and games. But when he gets a little older and finds a more challenging hobby, say, basketball, or golf, he naturally gives up his childish playthings. As one moves on, one finds this happening again and again. The point is this: As we age, we tend to progress, to replace youthful, fleeting enjoyments and commitments with those that are more mature and long-lasting.

Krishna here explains to Arjuna the importance of taking this principle to the next step, to mature spiritually. *Bhagavad-gita* is replete with guidelines for developing "a higher taste," thereby enabling one to rise beyond material desires. Gradually, by following the injunctions of the *Gita,* one can develop refined material tastes, and after that, spiritual life proper. Ultimately, *Bhagavad-gita* encourages giving up the temporary in favor of that which is eternal.

Killing Karma

In the *Gita's* third chapter, Krishna recommended both Karma-yoga (non-fruitive action) and *yajna* (sacrifice) as sure means to spiritual progress. Now, in the fourth chapter, Krishna takes us further, giving us a glimpse into knowledge of God, the *jiva* (individual soul), and their eternal relationship. He does this by giving a foretaste of what is to come: He explains both Jnana-yoga and Bhakti-yoga. And He explains how to rid oneself of karmic reactions.

Krishna begins by strongly asserting the necessity for oral transmission of spiritual knowledge, from master to disciple. He says that He began this system Himself many millions of years earlier, and that it continues on through disciplic succession (*parampara*). Because the ancient succession was broken, Krishna is now speaking the Gita again to Arjuna, who, as Krishna's devotee and friend, is qualified to understand "the transcendental mystery of this science" (4.1–3). I refer to these principles of transmission in the introduction to this work. It should be reiterated here that the principle of disciplic succession is essential to understand how the *Gita* is traditionally passed down and how it is meant to be received. According to Vaishnava teachings, the *Gita* can be understood on five different levels, each one more esoteric than the preceding. The initial level of understanding, which includes the distinction between matter and spirit and a fundamental perception of God and how He works, can be gleaned from a general reading of the *Gita*. However, there are "inner portions" or "secret (*guhya*) instructions" that are passed down in esoteric lineages, and these constitute the essence of the *Gita*'s most confidential message.

As chapter 4 continues, Krishna explains His transcendental nature as the Supreme Lord and the reason for His various "appearances," in the form of *avatars* ("divine descents"), in the mundane realm—He comes to reestablish religious principles when they are for some reason compromised (4.4–8). One who understands the transcendental nature of His appearance and activities, He says, attains liberation (4.9). Those who take shelter in Him are purified and happy, and they gradually achieve love for Him (4.10). He further informs Arjuna that He reciprocates with all souls in accordance with their degree of surrender and love (4.11).

As the *Gita* develops from here, Krishna elaborates upon the intricacies of action. He explains how transcendental knowledge allows one to become free from karmic debt. This occurs in the following way: A person who is spiritually learned—one who is in full knowledge of his spiritual nature and aware that he is subordinate to the Supreme—renounces self-interested actions and acts only for God. He is able to do this because he recognizes that everything belongs to God and should thus be used in His service. By practically applying this knowledge, he gradually becomes unaffected by the reactions of work. He becomes *karma*-free.

Krishna says that all Vedic knowledge is meant to bring one to this realization—that He is supreme and that all activity is meant for His pleasure. To help Arjuna come to this conclusion, He describes different types of sacrifice recommended in the *Vedas* (4.25–32) and states that they all culminate in transcendental knowledge (4.33). He then reveals the process for attaining such knowledge (by approaching a self-realized teacher), and He explains what that knowledge is—that all souls are part of Krishna (4.34–35). Transcendental knowledge destroys karmic reactions and brings attainment of "the supreme spiritual peace" (4.36–39). Those who never attain transcendental knowledge, however, attain neither happiness nor God consciousness (4.40). In conclusion, Krishna tells Arjuna to destroy his doubts by spiritual knowledge: "Armed with *yoga*," he tells Arjuna, "stand and fight" (4.41–42).

The idea of becoming relieved of *karma* may be the most important teaching here. While the *Gita* briefly addresses this subject, it is dealt with more systematically in later Vaishnava literature. Briefly, *karma* is described in three categories. (1) Prarabdha-karma refers to the reactions of past activities, including those from prior lives, that influence our present; (2) Sanchita-karma includes past activities as well, but the reactions will not manifest until our next life; and (3) Agami-karma, or Bija-karma, is current activity that will take effect later in this life or in a future one. The first two are irreversible, except by *bhakti,* or God's grace, but the last one can be reversed by a change in action.

In this sense, *karma* can be compared to golf. In Prarabdha- and Sanchita-karma you have already hit the ball. It is soaring through the sky, and it is simply a matter of time until it hits the green. The stage of Agami-karma, on the other hand, corresponds to the moment just prior to hitting the ball—you may change your mind, choose a different iron, or walk away from the game altogether.

In terms of broader categories, *karma* is again usually described as being of three types: (1) *Karma* refers to activities that are good but still material. Because these activities are good, they warrant a good reaction. Thus, they bind one to the material world—the world of good and evil. (2) *Vikarma* refers to bad activities. Naturally, if one performs such acts, one will accrue bad reactions. Again, this binds one to the material world. (3) *Akarma* refers to activities that carry no material reaction. They are spiritual acts with God in the center, and they are thus liberating. This is Karma-yoga.

As Wendy Doniger, professor of the history of religions at the University of Chicago, has written in *The Origins of Evil in Hindu Mythology:*

> . . . devotion to God can overcome *karma.* This simple faith has an elaborate, classical foundation in the philosophy of Ramanuja [eleventh century], who maintained that God could "even override the power of *karma* to draw repentant sinners to him." Thus the doctrine of *karma* is deeply determined by other important strains of Indian religion in which the individual is able to swim against the current of time and fate. (p. 16)

A. L. Herman sums up these points in *A Brief Introduction to Hinduism*:

> Karma-yoga, "the way of action," offers a way out of the problem of suffering by showing the path to actionless action, that is, a way of acting that does not produce karmic consequences. In other words, Karma-yoga produces actions without karmic residues. And if an action is without karmic residues then the law of *karma* will not reward the agent (in a temporary heaven or by a better birth in the next life) nor will it punish the agent (in a temporary hell or by a worse birth in the next life). The conclusion is that the problem of suffering is solved because the cause of *dukha* [distress], desire for the fruits of the act, is crushed by the *yoga* of actionless action, a *yoga* that leads ultimately to heaven and eternal peace in Lord Krishna. (p. 119)

Actionless Action

As the *Gita*'s fifth chapter opens, Arjuna wants clarification. Krishna has glorified knowledge and renunciation, and He has praised sacrificial work. But rather than telling Arjuna to study scripture, renounce the war, or work as a priest, He tells him to fight. Arjuna is again perplexed because Krishna is stressing what appears to him to be contradictory teachings—work in devotion and inaction in knowledge. Consequently, this chapter begins with Arjuna asking Krishna to state definitively which of the two paths is more beneficial (5.1). Arjuna is once again confused because, to him, work and renunciation appear incompatible. To clear up Arjuna's confusion, Krishna explains, in the fifth chapter, that devotional work in full knowledge has no material reaction and is therefore the same as (or even better than) renunciation of work (5.2).

At this point, Krishna decides to describe the type of people who have actually achieved this state, thus giving Arjuna a more tangible, practical way to understand what He is talking about: Krishna enumerates the characteristics of one who works in such an unattached, devotional manner, who sacrifices the fruits of work to God (5.3–17). Such a devotional *yogi*, purified by transcendental knowledge, realizes that he is a spiritual entity, Krishna says. Since he is transcendental to his body, mind, and senses, he does not identify with their actions. Performing actions and renouncing their fruits to the Supreme, he is "not affected by sinful action, as the lotus leaf is untouched by water" (5.10). Thus he attains total peacefulness. Such an unattached person becomes situated in transcendence. He is said to have perfect knowledge of the self and he develops love for the Supreme. He sees all beings with equal vision, and he understands their spiritual nature beyond the external, material body. Such a person works for the ultimate spiritual welfare of others and is unattached to the dualities of pleasure and pain. He is not attracted to material sense pleasure, but enjoys pleasure within, concentrating on God (5.18–29). His activities may appear like those of others, but they are worlds apart.

The description here of the self-realized soul is similar to the description of the *sthita-prajna* at the end of *Gita*'s second chapter. And Arjuna's confusion at the beginning of this chapter echoes his confusion in the beginning of chapter three. Vaishnava commentators say that these things are repeated for the sake of Arjuna's future audience, the readers of *Bhagavad-gita*. They say that Arjuna was himself a liberated soul, posing as one conditioned so that Krishna might reveal the teachings of the *Gita* for spiritual seekers throughout the world.

Yoga Means "To Link"

In the *Gita*'s sixth chapter, Krishna introduces a new subject: Dhyana-yoga, a meditative technique made popular today as Hatha-yoga. He mentions it to Arjuna because it was also popular in ancient times. Back then, it was called Raja-yoga, because great kings (*raja*) used to practice it to develop mystic powers. As we will see, however, Arjuna rejects it as the wrong method for this age. If one is going to link with God (*yoga* means "to link"), one needs the right tools for the job. The right process for the right time.

In golf, as in most other fields of endeavor, you need the right tools to play a good game. In this day and age, says Gary McCord, in his book *Golf for Dummies*, there's no excuse for having equipment ill-suited to your swing, body, and game. As far as choosing golf balls, clubs, bags, accessories—it's the difference between a successful game and, well, one that is not worth playing.

The same is true of *yoga*. To link with God, one needs the correct equipment, that is, yogic process. If one is serious about spiritual realization, says the *Gita*, one must bid adieu to popular *yoga* techniques, which are ineffective in this age (as Arjuna will soon tell us in chapter 6). Of course, these techniques may be useful for exercise and fitness purposes. But for God consciousness, one should hear what Krishna has to say. He is, after all, the founder of the *yoga* system, and the *Gita* is the original textbook on the subject.

In chapter 6 of the *Gita*, Krishna outlines the path of Dhyana-yoga (technically called Ashtanga-yoga, "the eight-fold path"), a mechanical practice meant to control the mind and senses. The ultimate goal here is to focus one's concentration on Paramatma ("Supersoul"), the form of Krishna within the heart. After stating the importance of controlling the mind (6.5–6), Krishna describes one who has done so—the *yogi*, or transcendentalist (6.7–9). Krishna then summarizes the methodology and ultimate goal of the Ashtanga-yoga system. Sitting postures, breathing exercises, and sense and mind control culminate in *samadhi,* or consciousness fixed on the Supersoul (6.10–19). One who has attained perfection in *yoga* has a steady mind, fixed on the Supreme. He is liberated, his mind is peaceful, his passions are quieted, he experiences "boundless transcendental happiness," and he is never disturbed, even in the midst of the greatest difficulties. He has spiritual perspective. Thus he is freed from all miseries resulting from the soul's contact with matter (6.20–32).

But to perform *yoga* properly, even for someone as qualified as Arjuna, is unlikely. Arjuna himself complains that the system of Ashtanga-yoga is too difficult to practice: "For the mind is restless, turbulent, obstinate, and very strong, O Krishna, and, it seems to me, controlling it would be more difficult than controlling the wind" (6.33–34). Krishna replies that controlling the mind is indeed difficult, but "it is possible by consistent practice and by detachment" (6.35–36). Ultimately, the *Gita*'s commentators reveal that Ashtanga-yoga was for a previous age, when people lived for "many hundreds of years." According to Patanjali's *Yoga-sutra*, it is a technique that takes at least a lifetime to perfect. And in this age, when people are distracted from spiritual life and life span is short, it is nearly impossible to practice it to perfection.

As golf pro Bob Arnold writes in his book *The Meditative Golfer:* "Golf is like sex and *yoga*—few do it in just the right way!" (p. 6).

Arjuna's next question reflects his skepticism about Ashtanga-yoga and the likelihood (or unlikelihood) of perfecting the technique in one lifetime. He inquires about the fate of the *yogi* who falls from *yoga* practice before reaching the goal (6.37–39). Krishna replies that an unsuccessful *yogi,* who passes away before completing the process, will take an auspicious birth, perhaps in a wealthy or pious family. He may even be born in a family of transcendentalists who are rich in wisdom. Whatever the case, Krishna says, he eventually resumes his practice and, after many such births, attains perfection (6.40–45). This applies not only to Ashtanga-yoga but to all endeavors directed toward God that remain incomplete after one lifetime. In fact, many of the principles Krishna describes in relation to Ashtanga-yoga can be applied to all *yoga* processes. For example, He tells Arjuna that one cannot be a *yogi* if one "eats too much or eats too little, sleeps too much or does not sleep enough" (6.16). *Yoga,* according to Krishna, is thus the perfect Middle Way—a balance between excess and unnecessary austerity—the culmination of an idea that is embraced in most forms of Buddhism.

The sixth chapter may be summed up as follows: "A *yogi* is greater than an empiricist, a fruitive worker, and an ascetic. Therefore, O Arjuna, in all circumstances, be a *yogi.* And of all *yogis,* the one who has faith in Me, worshiping Me in spirit and in a mood of loving service, is most intimately united with Me in *yoga* and is the best of all" (6.46–47).

Yoga (linking with the Supreme, whether on the golf links or anywhere else) is thus superior to asceticism (*tapasya*), fruitive work (*karma*), and empiricism (*jnana*). And of all paths of *yoga* (i.e., Karma-yoga, Jnana-yoga, Ashtanga-yoga, etc.), Bhakti-yoga (loving devotional service to Krishna) is declared by the *Gita* to be the highest.

4

Devotional Love:
The Name of the Game

I may be able to speak the languages of men and even of angels, but if I have no love, my speech is no more than a noisy gong or a clanging bell. I may have the gift of inspired preaching; I may have all knowledge and understand all secrets; I may have all the faith needed to move mountains— but if I have no love, I am nothing. I may give away everything I have, and even give up my body to be burned—but if I have no love, this does me no good.

—St. Paul, 1 Corinthians

In other words, the first and second ways [i.e., *karma* and *jnana*] both lead to the third [i.e., *bhakti*]. Love is the greatest of these ways. For in the end, grace comes from God, from the Authentic Self.

—Bagger Vance, 74

*L*ove. Few words are as pleasing or as powerful. From the biblical Song of Songs to Shakespeare's *Romeo and Juliet* and Wagner's *Tristan und Isolde,* themes of love permeate our culture. In the East, too, one finds the Islamic love classic, *Layla and Majnun,* and, farther east, the Rasa-lila of Radha and Krishna. The universal language of love transcends the limitations of culture and speech, of time and religion.

All living beings want to love and be loved. This desire is natural. And when it is not fulfilled, we find surrogates. A recent study was conducted on cats and dogs and humans as well: A mother cat deprived of her kittens might nurse a mouse, or a dog might care for a kitten. Similarly, a human with no natural object of affection may take in a dog or cat and love it as if it were her own child. Love there must be, but love for what, or for whom?

Abe Stark compares golf and love in his book *The Love of the Game:*

> I realized that golf and love have a lot in common. You need the right equipment for the game. If you go into either golf or love in a distracted way, you might as well not go in. You need discipline, determination, and a positive attitude—or your game or loved one will suffer. You need dedication; otherwise, you'll be a mediocre player on both fields. You've got to enjoy playing. Otherwise, what's the point? When you get into either golf or love, it's all-consuming. In fact, many a marriage has split over preoccupation with golf. (p. 76)

Love is all good, but sometimes it is misplaced. If love for a game ruins a marriage, it is obviously not doing what it is supposed to do. If love is centered on animals as opposed to (and not in addition to) humans, this is also questionable. Ultimately, love takes place between people, human beings who cherish each other in a wholesome and healthy way. Love is a deep appreciation for another to the point of making a commitment. It means wanting to act, to do something—anything—to care for, nurture, and fulfill the needs and desires of the beloved. It is an exchange of emotion that is fundamentally fulfilling.

When applied to God, it is called *bhakti.* According to the

Gita, loving exchange with God is the most natural repose of our loving propensity. After all, God is our source, our maintainer, our ultimate destination. No being is more intimately connected to us, or more concerned about our welfare.

While *bhakti* is the ultimate path articulated by Bagger Vance—as well as by Krishna—details are not to be found in Pressfield's novel. Junah expresses his high regard for Vance, but nowhere does he say that he loves Vance. Unlike Arjuna, who states outright that he loves Krishna with heart and soul (11.41–42), Junah appears to accept Vance's love without reciprocation.

Vance's love for Junah, on the other hand, is clear:

Vance's gaze regarded Junah with pure, limitless love. (p. 183)

More devoted than mother, more faithful than a lover, I stand by your side always. I will never abandon you. No sin, no lapse, no crime, however heinous, can make me desert you, nor yield up to you any less than my ultimate fidelity and love. (pp. 185–86)

The latter part of this statement is similar to Krishna's declaration of dedication to His devotee: "Out of love, I protect My devotee from all sinful reaction" (18.66).

Junah's silence regarding his love for Vance, if it indeed exists, might be traced to a type of impersonalism, a subject I will explore more fully in later sections of the *Gita.*

Briefly, if God is not a person, how can one love Him? This question is nicely explored by Professor Lee Siegel in his book *The Sacred and Profane Dimensions of Love in Indian Traditions as Exemplified in the Gita-govinda of Jayadeva,* where he points out that the impersonal Brahman

cannot be loved because the very idea of *brahman* precludes
any idea of love, of distinction between subject and object,
lover and beloved. Love as a force which "couples or seeks to
couple some two things" into one cannot exist because there
is no two-ness, only unity. Love is quite irrelevant. (p. 13)

Exactly how love or devotion (*bhakti*) plays a part in the
theology of the *Gita* is the main point of its middle six chapters, which I will now analyze in some depth.

——— "Of Golfers, I Am Tiger Woods . . ." ———

The distinction between spirit and matter has been estab-
lished in the *Gita*'s first six chapters. The living entity has
been described as a nonmaterial, spiritual person existing
in a material body. The *Gita* further describes that this spiritual person is able to liberate himself from material self-
identification through different types of *yoga*. These *yoga*
systems—including Ashtanga, Karma, and Jnana—are like a
"*yoga* ladder" culminating in Bhakti-yoga (devotion to
Krishna).

The middle section of the *Gita* (chapters 7 through 12) is
concerned with Krishna and His eternal relationship with
the spiritual entities mentioned above—which refers to each
one of us. This relationship is based on loving devotion, and
thus seers of the Vaishnava tradition say these middle six
chapters primarily deal with Bhakti-yoga, although many
tangential points are made as well.

The seventh chapter of the *Gita* begins by explaining how
the ultimate end of knowledge is knowledge about love of

Krishna. It also explains the process of attaining that knowledge. The first three verses give us a glimpse of the entire chapter. In these verses He tells Arjuna: "Full knowledge of Me only comes to those who are devoted to Me with love. Although I shall now grant you all material and spiritual knowledge, you should know that knowledge of Me, specifically, is confidential and rarely attained. This too shall I give to you."

Knowledge of Krishna begins with knowledge of His energies: the "inferior" energy (matter), consisting of eight material elements—earth, water, fire, air, and ether (as well as mind, intelligence, and the subtle form of ego that allows one to misidentify with the body)—and His "superior" energy (spirit), which includes us, the many living entities now existing in the material world (7.4–5).

Krishna tells Arjuna that He is the "origin and dissolution" of both energies—He is their ultimate source and their final destination (7.6–7). Having explained this, Krishna delineates how one can see Him within all phenomena: He is "the original fragrance of the earth, the heat in fire . . . taste of water, the light of the sun and the moon . . . the intelligence of the intelligent," and so on (7.8–12). Krishna identifies Himself with the best of all possible things—the first in any category. He will do this again in the tenth chapter: "Of bodies of water I am the ocean . . . of immovable things I am the Himalayas. . . . Of all creations, I am the beginning, middle, and end. Of letters I am the letter A. . . . Of all sciences, I am the transcendent science of the Self, and among logicians I am the conclusive truth." Pressfield missed an opportunity in the Bagger Vance version. He could have had Vance say, "Of golfers I am Tiger Woods."

───────── **Four Kinds of Gamesmen** ─────────

In golf, there's a thing called "a foursome" or, sometimes, "a four-ball." Basically, this just means that golf is usually played with three other people. One tends to play in two teams of two. Not that this has anything to do with the *Gita*. But Krishna also seems to think of groups in terms of "four-somes." In the next few verses of the seventh chapter, for example, He mentions four kinds of people who tend to avoid spiritual life, and then He mentions four kinds who embrace it (7.15–18). Briefly, those who veer away from the spirit are (1) the foolish or ignorant; (2) gross sensualists; (3) intelligent individuals whose knowledge is stolen by illusion; and (4) those who are just plain evil. The four types of people who do become devotees, Krishna says, are (1) those who are distressed and looking for answers to life's many questions; (2) people who want wealth, both material and spiritual; (3) the sincerely inquisitive; and (4) those who earnestly search for the truth. He especially favors the last of these four.

Krishna says that when one becomes a devotee, for what-ever reason, one becomes wise, knowing Him to be the supreme cause of everything. Thus, devotees are people who surrender unto Him, and the fruits of their surrender are deep and lasting (7.19). Materialists, on the other hand, surrender to demigods (whether mythic beings or contem-porary celebrities) to attain immediate fruitive benefits, which are limited and temporary (7.20–23). Krishna tells us that impersonalists, or those who emphasize His imper-sonal feature, are subject to illusions similar to those expe-rienced by outright materialists. By His own mystic potency,

He keeps His personal form concealed from them, for they offend Him by denying His personal feature (7.24–26).

Here again we see Krishna disparage the impersonalist conception of the Supreme. Vaishnava teachers, following Krishna's lead, feel personally offended when their beautiful Lord is described as having no eyes, no mouth, no hair, and, sometimes, no love. To deny God these distinct personal characteristics, they say, is the height of arrogance. Do humans have something that God does not? Would this not make us greater than Him? Especially when it comes to loving exchange. We can love, but God cannot?

Professor Huston Smith expresses these ideas with the help of a traditional poem by Tukaram, a Maharashtrian mystic-poet:

> As healthy love is out-going, the *bhakta* will reject all suggestions that the God one loves is oneself, even one's deepest Self, and insist on God's otherness. As a Hindu devotional classic puts the point, "I want to taste sugar; I don't want to be sugar."

> Can water quaff itself?
> Can trees taste of the fruit they bear?
> He who worships God must stand distinct from Him,
> So only shall he know the joyful love of God;
> For if he say that God and he are one,
> That joy, that love, shall vanish instantly away.

> Pray no more for utter oneness with God:
> Where were the beauty if jewel and setting were one?
> The heat and the shade are two,
> If not, where were the comfort of shade?
> Mother and child are two,
> If not, where were the love?
> When after being sundered, they meet,

What joy do they feel, the mother and child!
Where were joy, if the two were one?
Pray, then, no more for utter oneness with God. (p. 33)*

In the final four verses of chapter 7, Krishna concludes that those who are pious and intelligent and who aspire for liberation seek refuge in Him through the process of devotional service, knowing Him to be Supreme.

——— Death: It's Par for the Course ———

The eighth chapter of the *Gita* focuses on the moment of death—it explains how to approach this most bewildering and frightening moment with dignity and spiritual clarity. At the beginning of the chapter, Arjuna asks Krishna a series of questions: "Arjuna inquired: O Lord, O Supreme God, what is this spiritual substance called 'Brahman'? What is *karma?* What is the material world? And what are demigods? Please explain this to me. How does the Lord of sacrifice reside in the body, and in which part does He live? And how can those engaged in acts of devotion know You at the time of death?" (8.1–2). Krishna gives a brief response to the first six questions (8.3–4)—these are subjects He had addressed earlier at length. But He replies to the last question (concerning remembrance of Him at the time of death) with extra emphasis, perhaps because of its importance to a man who is, after all, on a battlefield. Further, battlefield or not, death is something we must all face, sooner or later, and so Krishna spends the rest of this chapter explaining in

*Song by Tukaram, trans. John S. Hoyland in *An Indian Peasant Mystic* (1932; reprint, Richmond, Ind.: Prinit Press, 1978).

detail how one can think of Him at this most crucial juncture in one's sojourn in the material world.

Krishna tells Arjuna that whoever dies while remembering Him will be peaceful and attain His abode (8.5). The state of one's consciousness at the time of death, Krishna says, will determine one's next body (8.6). Since one's thoughts and memories at death are influenced by one's consciousness and activities during life, Krishna instructs Arjuna to think of Him constantly, even in the course of his prescribed duties (8.7–8). This brings to mind a conversation I had with my rabbi when I was very young. He told me that the Shma, a famous prayer central to the Jewish faith, should be chanted the day before one dies. "How is it possible?" I asked him. "We don't know which day we will die." The rabbi was pleased. "Precisely," he said. "Therefore, the Jewish people recite this prayer on a daily basis."

Everyone must die—That's par for the course. But a life of devotion is a life well lived. By meditating on Krishna constantly, one can lead a full life in this world and join Him after quitting the body. In verse 9, Krishna gives explicit directions for how one should meditate on Him:

> [He should be seen as] the one who has complete knowledge of everything, who is the original living being, the controller of all existence, and the universal maintainer of the entire cosmos. He is inconceivable, and He always has personal characteristics. He is luminous like the sun and totally transcendental to material nature.

Krishna then describes the difficult system of Ashtanga-yoga yet again, explaining how this can lead to the attainment of higher planets (8.11–13). He concludes, however, that He is more easily and directly attained by one who has unflinching devotion for Him (8.14). Thus the *Gita's* middle section again brings the subject back to *bhakti.* After reaching Krishna in the spiritual world, the devotee never returns to the material world, which is subject to birth, death, old age, and disease (8.15–16).

Beyond the material world, which is perpetually created and destroyed, is the transcendental world, Krishna's eternal and supreme abode. The *Gita* explains that there are various heavenly planets, and above those are the Vaikuntha planets, or the kingdom of God. Upon attaining any of the Vaikuntha planets—and especially Krishna's supreme abode—one never returns to the material world (8.17–21). One attains this supreme destination, Krishna reiterates, by pure devotion (8.22). Next, Krishna describes how different kinds of *yogis* leave their bodies at particular auspicious moments to attain elevation to celestial planets, or even liberation. The devotee, however, is not concerned with such processes—he or she wants only pure devotion for Krishna (8.23–27). The eighth chapter finishes with Krishna's promise that His devotee achieves all the benefits of other systems of spiritual advancement. Ultimately, He says, at the time of death the devotee returns to Him in the spiritual world (8.28).

——— **In the Kingdom of Bagger Vance** ———

In the beginning of the ninth chapter, Krishna says that He will now impart "the highest form of education. The most confidential of all secrets. It is the purest knowledge, and because it gives direct perception of the self, it is the perfection of religion. It has eternal value and it is always performed with great bliss" (9.1–3). This refers to Sanatana-dharma, or the soul's primary function as an eternal servant of Krishna. In essence, this is *bhakti,* and Krishna will return to this by the end of the chapter. But first, Krishna reminds Arjuna that the whole cosmic creation rests within Him, that He is the source, maintainer, and controller of the universe (9.4–10). Krishna next reiterates His point about impersonalists. He says that only fools deride His personal humanlike form, and He contrasts them with the great souls (*mahatmas*), aware of His divinity, who worship Him with devotion (9.11–14). These great souls, He says, are always chanting His glories. The genuine Vaishnava lineages, therefore, stress the importance of chanting the Holy Name of the Lord, and they recommend it as the chief means of realization in this age. Mantra Yoga—devotional hymns, *japa* (soft chanting on beads), *kirtan* (joyous singing of God's Names)—is thus the central practice for those who follow the *Gita's* teachings.

Krishna then decides to elaborate on different types of worshipers—worshipers of impersonal Brahman, of demigods, and of the universal form—and He describes Himself as the actual and ultimate object of worship, the protector of His devotees, and the ultimate beneficiary of all sacrifices to the demigods (9.23–24). Here the *Gita* asserts a strong monotheistic message. Krishna acknowledges that, for various reasons, people worship lesser gods, powerful administrators of universal affairs. But He says that those who have actual knowledge worship Him alone, for He is the Supreme Personality of Godhead. In His own words:

> But it is I who am the ritual, I the sacrifice, the offering to the ancestors, the healing herb, the spiritual chant. I am both the butter and the fire of the offering. I am the father

of the universe, the mother, the support, and the grandsire. I am the object of knowledge, the purifier of everything, and the mystical syllable om. I am also the embodiment of the *Vedas*. I am the goal, the sustainer, the master, the witness, the abode, the refuge and the most dear friend. I am the creation and the annihilation, the basis of everything, the resting place and the eternal seed. (9.16–18)

He goes on to describe His supremacy in various other ways, and concludes by offering Arjuna these assuring words: Other worshipers attain the abodes of their objects of worship, but "those who worship Me will live with Me" (9.25).

Does Junah go to Vance after death? Given the parameters of *The Legend of Bagger Vance,* one wonders where Vance came from, and where he goes after his current incarnation is finished. Of course, Vance is a fictional character, but details of his "past" and his probable "future" would be intriguing. In Pressfield's novel, Vance mysteriously and suddenly appears. And, just as quickly, he disappears. A follow-up book could be written about Vance's background. It would be interesting to learn about his home planet, or at least about his early years on this one. Many books have been written about the "eighteen missing years" of Jesus' life, and some have even theorized that he visited India. Vance, as noted earlier, did in fact travel to India, and details would be illuminating.

It would also be interesting to learn more about Junah. Just how was his life changed after his meeting with Bagger Vance? Did he tell others about his supernatural experience? Did he become a dedicated devotee? Did he spread Vance's message of the Authentic Swing to people who were interested?

In the final verses of the *Gita*'s ninth chapter, Krishna talks about His devotees. By making Him the object of all actions, offerings, and austerities, His devotee is freed from the bondage of *karma* and attains Him (9.26–28). Although in one sense impartial, regarding all living beings equally, Krishna naturally favors those who serve Him in loving devotion (9.29). Even if a devotee acts inappropriately, he is still to be considered saintly, since he is, after all, a devotee, and is thus "properly situated." Gradually, Krishna says, the process of devotional service will elevate him to righteousness and perfection (9.30–31). In conclusion, Krishna declares that one who is completely devoted to Him attains Him: "Engage your mind always in thinking of Me, become My devotee, engage your body in My service, and surrender unto Me. Completely absorbed in Me, without doubt you will come to Me" (9.34). Thus, the ninth chapter ultimately concludes with an endorsement of devotional service.

The "Nutshell" Verses

In the tenth chapter, Krishna explains the essence of the *Gita* in four "nutshell" verses. But first, to instill further devotion, He explains His specific opulences, which are manifested in His all-pervasive energies. He begins by asserting that those who are wise, knowing Him as the Supreme Lord and the original source of everything, are freed from all reactions to sins. They engage themselves in pure, devotional service to Him, without any separate motive or agenda (10.2–8). The unique characteristics of such pure devotees are then described (10.9). Krishna says that he dispels any ignorance they may have and leads them to Him (10.10–11).

Verses 8 through 11 are the four "nutshell" verses:

> I am the source of all material and spiritual universes. Everything comes from Me. The wise who perfectly know this engage in My devotional service and worship Me from the core of their being (10.8). The thoughts of My pure devotees always focus on Me, their lives are fully devoted to My service, and they derive great bliss and happiness from enlightening one another and conversing about me (10.9). To those who are perpetually devoted to serving me with love, I give the understanding by which they can come to Me (10.10). To show them special mercy, I, who dwell in their hearts, destroy with the shining lamp of knowledge the darkness that comes from ignorance. (10.11)

These four verses, in seven broad strokes, sum up the message of the *Gita:* (1) Krishna is the origin of everything. (2) Those who are wise thus engage in His loving service. (3) They always think of Him and (4) discuss His attributes—and this (5) brings them great pleasure. To such pure devotees, (6) Krishna gives full enlightenment, and concomitantly (7) destroys their ignorance.

In a conversation with Steven Pressfield, I asked him to enumerate four of Vance's teachings that he considered most important—a sort of Bagger Vance counterpart to the four nutshell verses of the *Gita.* He gave me the following list:

1. *The Search for the Authentic Swing.* "The search for the Authentic Swing is a parallel for the search for the Self."

2. *You Are Never Alone.* "Forget all else, Junah, but remember this: You are never alone. You have your caddie. You have me."

3. *The Field and the Knower.* "See how the player's will searches the Field and finds his Authentic Swing. . . . Now see him harmonize with it. Not until then does he begin his Swing in physicality."

4. *Don't Cheat.* "The greatness of this is that it mirrors Higher Reality. There can be no cheating in the dimension in which the Self resides. There every action inexorably produces a result, every thought its consequence."

Theologically, Pressfield is saying that (1) self-realization is important, and that one should pursue it; (2) that one is never alone—God always accompanies one in one's heart; (3) that until one gets in touch with one's own inner nature, with one's spiritual dimension, one never truly lives or makes proper use of one's God-given body; and (4) that the universal law of cause and effect (*karma*) will teach us every step of the way. Cheating is not possible—for we always get what is coming to us, in one way or another.

After Krishna reveals the four nutshell verses to Arjuna, the mighty bowman declares his total acceptance of Krishna as the Supreme. He further acknowledges as true all that Krishna has said (10.12–15).

Now a fully surrendered soul, Arjuna requests Krishna to describe His divine opulences in more detail (10.16–18). Krishna acquiesces, and His description of His principal opulences continues to the conclusion of the chapter. This is reminiscent of the list in chapter 7: Of lights He is the radiant sun, of bodies of water the ocean, of immovable things the Himalayas. He is the wisdom of the wise, the strength of the strong, the splendor of the splendid. All wondrous phenomena manifesting great power, beauty, grandeur, and sublimeness, in the material or spiritual world, are simply fragmental manifestations of His divine energies and opulence. Krishna, thus being the cause of all causes, is the supreme object of worship for all beings (10.19–41). In the final verse, He reveals to Arjuna that more important than all these specifics is the fact that everything exists merely because He enters into it—it is His essence that gives all of reality its existence.

The Universal Form

In the eleventh chapter of the *Gita,* Krishna directly reveals His "universal form"—a mystical image in which all of creation appears at once. This is the revelation by which Krishna "shows" His Godhood to Arjuna. The chapter begins with Arjuna's declaration that he is now freed from illusion. He attributes this to Krishna's mercy, to everything He has explained to him and shown him. He knows Krishna is Supreme, and he knows what he now must do on the battlefield. However, despite his certainty of Krishna's divinity and his confidence about his own course of action, he fears that others, in the future, may misunderstand. He therefore requests Krishna: "O greatest of all beings, O supreme person, though I see You here before me in Your actual form, I wish to see You as this cosmic manifestation. I wish to see that form of Yours" (11.3). To establish that Krishna is God beyond the shadow of a doubt, Arjuna requests Him to reveal His gigantic form of everything in existence (11.2–4). Krishna agrees to do this and grants Arjuna divine vision, enabling him to see it (11.5–8).

Krishna then reveals the spectacular, inconceivable form (11.9–49). Viewing it with astonishment, Arjuna sees that "everything—moving and nonmoving—is here completely, all in one place (11.7) . . . the unlimited expansions of the universe, all at once, although divided into many, untold thousands" (11.13). He sees "unlimited mouths, eyes, and wonderful visions. . . . All are inconceivable, brilliant, and ever-expanding" (11.11). Arjuna, his hairs standing on end, describes the vast and effulgent form and offers prayers of glorification (11.14–25).

He also sees in the universal form the entire opposing army, along with his own soldiers, rushing into a surrealistic image of Krishna's many mouths, meeting their doom (11.26-30). Unable to accommodate this vision, Arjuna urgently begs Krishna to explain this aspect of the great form (11.31). To this, Krishna replies that the outcome of the war is already set, and its manifestation is only separated by time: nearly all the soldiers present will be killed in the battle. He also informs Arjuna that although this will ultimately be the case with or without him, Arjuna should act as Krishna's instrument in the great fight and thus be assured of victory (11.32–34). Arjuna, overwhelmed, glorifies Krishna as the original master, the refuge of the universe and the cause of all causes (11.35–40). He begs Krishna to forgive him for his familiar dealings in the past, since he did not realize the extent of Krishna's divinity (11.41–44).

The Bagger Vance parallel is equally moving. Vance tells Junah that only he will be able to see his mystic form, because of "the divine eye" that Vance gives to him. Vance informs his worthy companion that, without this divine eye, the vision would cause his demise.

And then Junah saw it:

> [Unlimited] limbs and mouths. Now the world opened, the continents cracked. It was all Vance. Vance in some horrific cosmic form rending the earth as if it were a bauble. The planet was merely an atom to him. Less than an atom. In the maws of his countless mouths, the warriors in all their valor fell and perished. (p. 182)

Hardy, the narrator, who was nearby when Vance revealed his magnificent form to Junah, mentions that "the hair stood up on my neck" (p. 174), and later that "the hair stood straight up on my forearms" (p. 184). Truth is, Vance gave Hardy a vision of it, too, and, as Hardy describes it, "the bottom blew out of the world" (p. 127). One can only imagine the effect the cosmic revelation had on Junah. As for Arjuna, the *Gita* records that his hair stood erect as well (see above).

On July 16, 1946, Robert Oppenheimer, director of the Los Alamos Project in New Mexico, also felt his hair stand on end. For him, Krishna's universal form is similar to the first atomic blast, which occurred on that day. As a prominent figure in the development of atomic power and an important beneficiary of its success, he waited with anticipation for the testing of the first bomb. An observer who watched him that morning was quoted in Ted Single's book *The Ultimate Moment:*

He grew tenser as the seconds ticked off. He scarcely breathed. He held on to a post to steady himself. . . . When the announcer shouted "Now!" and there came this tremendous burst of light, followed . . . by the deep-growling roar of the explosion, his face relaxed in an expression of tremendous relief. (p. 15)

Devastated by the blast, Oppenheimer sat back in a stupor as he uttered two *Gita* verses related to the universal form: "I am all-devouring death" (10.34) and "I am Time, the great destroyer of all worlds, and I have come to take everyone and everything" (11.32). He was deeply disturbed by the evil potential of his accomplishments. But the atomic age was not to be held back, and it was now under way with full force. Arjuna, too, was disturbed by the magnitude of Krishna's universal image, and he anxiously asked Krishna to return to His more familiar form (11.45–46). But, unlike Arjuna, Oppenheimer cannot go back.

After informing Arjuna that he was the first person to have ever seen this universal form (11.47–48), Krishna resumes first His four-armed Vishnu form and then finally His original two-armed form, thus pacifying Arjuna, His devotee and friend (11.49–51).

Krishna then explains that His beautiful two-armed form is His most confidential feature, His original aspect, inconceivable even to the demigods. It is beyond understanding by Vedic study, penance, charity, and worship (11.52–53). Krishna concludes the chapter by declaring that His transcendental, humanlike form can be directly understood only by pure devotional service *(bhakti)* and that pure devotees, who are "friendly to every living entity," attain His eternal association (11.54–55).

———————— *Bhakti:* The Ultimate Goal ————————

Up to this point, Krishna has explained various conceptions of God—personal, impersonal, and even the universal form. He has also delineated the different *yoga* systems for approaching Him in His various manifestations. In the twelfth chapter, however, He directly reveals that Bhakti-yoga, devotional love and service directed to His personal form, is the highest and also most practical process of spiritual realization. He further outlines the superlative characteristics of those who become such lovers of God.

Arjuna again wants to be certain that he is understanding Krishna correctly. He does not question that worship of Krishna's personal form is the highest path and that devotion to Him is the best of all *yogas*. But he wants confirmation. In the first verse, therefore, he asks Krishna to state whom He considers more perfect—those engaged in His devotional service or the worshipers of the unmanifest Brahman, the impersonal, all-pervasive feature of God (12.1). Krishna replies: "He whose mind is focused on My personal form, always worshiping Me with great, spiritual faith, is considered by Me to be most perfect" (12.2).

Krishna does not mince words. He tells Arjuna that the worshipers of the impersonal Absolute eventually achieve Him, but it is much more difficult for them (12.3–5). He assures Arjuna that for those fixed in pure devotion to Him, He is "the swift deliverer from the ocean of birth and death" (12.6–7). It is for this reason that He instructs Arjuna to fix his mind and intelligence on Him and, by this simple method, attain Him (12.8).

For those unable to fix their attention upon Him in a

spontaneous and uninterrupted way, Krishna explains an indirect process by which they will gradually be able to. He says that they can begin with the cultivation of knowledge (*jnana*), and then proceed to meditation (*dhyana*). After that, they may learn to renounce the fruits of action (*karmaphala-tyaga*), to engage the fruits of work in His service (Karma-yoga), and finally to execute the regulative principles of Bhakti-yoga (*sadhana-bhakti*) (12.9–12). Thus, the *Gita* reveals a process by which anyone who wants to attain the Supreme may do so in due course.

Krishna concludes chapter 12 with a heartening description of the qualities and characteristics of His pure devotees, affirming at the end of each description that such devotees "are very dear to Me." These devotees are dear because they are free from material desires, material dualities, and false ego (or the identification with the body)—and because they are totally devoted to Krishna with great affection. Because Krishna has become their primary focus and supreme goal, they lovingly engage in His service with determination and faith.

5

Putting Knowledge First

"What do you know of life?" Bagger Vance stood before the champion. "Are you a god that you have plumbed the depths of existence's meaning? What statement can you make about what is real or important? Have you pierced the veil?"

—Bagger Vance, 96

I shall now explain to you all knowledge in full—both material and spiritual—and when you know this, there shall remain nothing further to be known.

—Lord Krishna to Arjuna, *Bhagavad-gita* 7.2

K nowledge and devotion are interrelated. To be truly devoted, one must have some understanding or knowledge about one's object of devotion. And if one is really devoted to someone or something, one's knowledge of that person or thing will naturally increase. Take golf, for example. Those who are devoted to the game are those who know the game best. And by their incessant playing and commitment to the green, they are constantly learning more and more about the world of golf.

The relationship between knowledge and devotion is the

central theme of the *Gita*'s final six chapters. These chapters show that the culmination of all knowledge and understanding involves developing devotion for the Supreme. In coming to this conclusion, however, the chapters take a somewhat circuitous route. They begin by explaining the Knower and the Field (the soul and the body), and how these two relate to God. The chapters then launch into an elaborate discussion of the three modes of material nature—goodness, passion, and ignorance—explaining how these three components of reality impact on everything we see, hear, feel, taste, and touch. Krishna explains these things with special attention to how they affect us in day-to-day life, thus offering a depthful psychological study of the living being as he relates to the material world around him. This is in keeping with the *jnana,* or knowledge, emphasis of these final six chapters, for what we know and how it affects us are important elements of our mental constitution.

Krishna then presents an analogy in which the material world is viewed as a mysterious banyan tree, with roots shooting upward while its branches are facing down—the opposite of a normal tree. This Zen-like image is meant to provoke thought about the inverted nature of material existence, and how it is merely a perverted reflection of the spiritual world. Thus, by encouraging us to contemplate earthly existence in a deeper way, seeing it as but a partial, shadow-like representation of ultimate truth, Krishna again pushes the envelope, as it were, broadening our *jnana* to accommodate a higher reality.

After this, He describes the various kinds of people in the world, and He analyzes why they do the things they do. He shows us how all activity relates to the modes of nature,

and how people can be understood by the types of austerities they perform, the types of food they eat, and so on. This
completes Krishna's psychological study of man in the
material world, after which He concludes His teaching by
stressing the importance of renunciation and devotion to
God. The above is an overview of what one will find in these
final six chapters. I will now explain these points in more
detail, always keeping in mind their connection to Jnana-
yoga. We can begin, in fact, by quoting Huston Smith's brief
summation of this rigorous discipline:

> Jnana-yoga, intended for spiritual aspirants who have a
> strong reflective bent, is the path to oneness with the God-
> head through knowledge. Such knowledge—the Greeks' *gno-
> sis* and *sophia*—has nothing to do with factual information;
> it is not encyclopedic. It is, rather, an intuitive discernment
> that transforms. . . . Thinking is important for such people.
> They live in their heads a lot because ideas have for them an
> almost palpable vitality; they dance and sing for them.
> (p.29)

———————— **Heads above the Rest** ————————

If a person practicing Jnana-yoga tends to live in his head,
as Smith points out, then Junah starts out as something of a
jnani, for Vance is constantly trying to get him to go beyond
his mental involvement:

> You're in your head, Junah. I need you to come down into
> your hands. Listen to me. Intelligence, I have told you, does
> not reside in the brain but in the hands. Let them do the
> thinking, they're far wiser than you are. Be patient. Let the
> club settle. Don't make a move toward the ball until the

leather has found its proper nestle. Remember, the hands do not create the swing, they *find* it, they *remember* it. Do you recall in the East how the *sadhus* would sit, palms upturned in contemplation, making antennas of their hands? The golfer's hands are his antennas too, searching the Field, drawing in the Authentic Swing. (p. 119)

On one level, the idea here is similar to what Krishna has been telling Arjuna all along. "Don't be in your head, be in the world. Don't be cerebral, be practical. Don't give up work—instead, work for Me." Going off to the Himalayas and contemplating one's navel might seem exotic and spiritual—but it is not real *yoga*. Most return after a short time and resume materialistic activity. Rather—with the exception of a precious few who can engage the mind in rigorous study and discipline—*yoga* is best accomplished by doing something practical for God (while cultivating meditational techniques meant to assist this end). One gets closer to God by acting, not merely by meditating. In Arjuna's case, it was fighting. In Junah's, it was letting go and just playing the game.

Of course, Vance's main point here is "letting go." He implies that one can get too mental, too caught up in *trying* to focus, thus losing one's natural and almost simple ability to do so. Fact is, it is almost impossible to do something if you think it into the ground. The same is true in *yoga*. A beginner may have to learn technique and, perhaps all-too-self-consciously, follow the masters. But if he becomes dependent on this as he becomes more adept, he misses the point of *yoga*. He needs to reach a point where he can let go, where he can spontaneously act for God, without reservation, without caution. He must become free. And, in becoming free, he becomes bound in love.

———————— **A Whole New Playing Field** ————————

The thirteenth chapter of *Bhagavad-gita* focuses primarily on the interrelationship between the body, the soul, and the Supersoul (Paramatma). As the chapter opens, Arjuna inquires about six depthful subjects: material nature, the enjoyer of nature, the Field, the Knower of the Field, knowledge, and the ultimate conclusion of knowledge (13.1). In essence, he mainly wants to know about enjoyment and exactly how it works—Who enjoys, humans or God? What is enjoyment? When is it appropriate to enjoy? All this talk of knowledge and renunciation is frightening—what about just enjoying ourselves in the real world?

Krishna begins by reiterating the basics of spiritual knowledge. The body is known as *kshetra,* says Krishna, which is Sanskrit for "the Field of action." This Field, according to the *Gita,* consists of twenty-four material elements, including earth, water, fire, air, ether, mind, and intelligence, as well as more subtle phenomena, such as conviction and desire. The soul, or the actual person in the body, is known as *kshetra-jna,* Sanskrit for "the Knower of the Field of activities" (13.2).

Beyond the *kshetra-jna* (the individual knower of the body, or the soul), is the ultimate *kshetra-jna* (the Supersoul, or God)—the supreme knower of all facets of existence. Thus, the *Gita* teaches about the body (the Field), the soul (the Knower of the Field), and God (Supersoul), and it is very clear about the distinction between these three.

Perhaps I'm mistaken, but in the *Bagger Vance* book these three seem to merge. It might be me. Having read monistic interpretations of the *Gita* that tend to overlook the distinctions between the body, the soul, and God—saying that all existence is basically one absolute truth—it might be that I'm incorrectly applying these ideas to the teachings of Bagger Vance, reading into his words a reality that doesn't really exist there. Let's look at this a little more closely.

Unless I misunderstand him, Vance says that enlightenment is attained when "the Knower" becomes identical with "the Field." In his own words, "Only when the Knower and the Field are one do they swing" (p. 133). Vance also seems to merge the Knower of the Field (the soul) and God: He tells Junah, "I am your Self, the Ground of your being, your Authentic Swing" (p. 186). Is Vance talking about literal "oneness" or a sort of "oneness in purpose," oneness in an abstract, mystical sense? From the text itself, it is hard to tell.

———— (There's a) Hole in One(ness) ————

There is a tradition of *Gita* commentaries—originating from what is referred to as the monistic school of thought, where the impersonal, formless absolute is emphasized, and the Personality of Godhead, Krishna, is played down—that takes "oneness with God" quite literally. Such commentaries promote merging with the Supreme. So, again, when Bagger Vance talks about the two becoming one, is he supporting monistic literalism, or is he speaking metaphorically?

The impersonal or monistic conception of the Supreme—wherein one merges with ultimate but formless reality—is a legitimate part of what the *Gita* teaches. But it is only a part, and it is eclipsed by the idea of God as the Supreme Person. Despite the *Gita*'s emphasis on God's personhood, the impersonalistic dimension of the *Gita* has become more popular. Just why that is, I don't know. Vaishnava teachers suggest that the desire to depersonalize God comes, on a subliminal level, from the desire to avoid surrender: After all, if God is a person, then questions of submission and sub-servience come into play. If He is a formless abstraction, we can philosophize about Him without a sense of commit-ment, without the fear of having to acknowledge our duty to a higher being. Then again, maybe the popularity of the impersonal conception, at least in relation to the *Gita,* can be traced to inadequate knowledge of Sanskrit, plain and simple.

But if one reads the *Gita* according to Vaishnava tradi-tion, it becomes clear that it is the person Krishna, or Bha-gavan, who reigns Supreme, and who is emphasized by the disciplic lineages. The *Gita* itself supports the personalistic doctrine: Krishna says, "I am at the basis of the impersonal Brahman [i.e., the formless Absolute]" (14.27). And, when discussing the comparative value of the impersonal and the personal, He says, "Those who focus their minds on My per-sonal form, always engaged in worshiping Me with intense spiritual faith, are considered by Me to be most perfect" (12.2). In other words, the conception of God as a person, to Whom one may become devoted, is prior and superior to the conception of God as an impersonal force, into which one may merge—at least according to the *Gita.*

──────────── Enjoying the Game? ────────────

Back to the subject of the Supersoul, or the ultimate Knower of the Field. Although He exists as one, He appears separately in all bodies and within each atom (as the sun, although one, may simultaneously appear, in reflection, in various reservoirs of water). He is an expansion of Krishna, who manifests as the indwelling Lord, and by entering into all existence, He gives it life (13.3–7). Thus, again, the *Gita* carries a strong monotheistic message, as well as one that endorses a type of animism, pantheism, and panentheism— God is one but He also exists in nature and nature in Him.

The *Gita* explains that this manifestation of God as the Supersoul accompanies the individual soul, from body to body, as a friend and witness. He is the permitter of all activity and the maintainer of all beings.

The *Gita* gives more information on these two kinds of "Knowers of the Field" (individual souls and God). It says that the individual souls—such as you and I—are fallible, being subject to the degrading influences of material nature. These influences, the *Gita* tells us, include various kinds of illusion that culminate in misidentification with the body, which, in turn, lead to lust, anger, and greed. The Supersoul, on the other hand, is infallible, for God is immune to matter's influence.

Krishna then discusses the importance of attaining true knowledge, enumerating items that fit into this category. He includes among these humility, tolerance, nonviolence, self-control, nonattachment, a peaceful disposition, and unalloyed devotion to Him. These qualities (and the others He briefly mentions) are the stuff of goodness—and the *Gita* not only encourages that one develop these qualities but explains just how to do so. Krishna further says that the process of attaining knowledge facilitates the embodied souls' liberation from matter (13.8–12).

Krishna next describes the essence of all that can be

known—*jneya* ("the knowable"). He asserts that all knowledge is properly perceived only by realizing the Supersoul, who exists in all moving and nonmoving things, for the Lord in this form is the true source of everything that exists. As its source, He knows all things thoroughly and permeates these things as their very essence. Thus, knowing Him in truth includes knowledge of everything else.

Accordingly, Krishna elaborates on the Supersoul's nature: "He is the source of light in all luminous objects. He is beyond the darkness of matter and is unmanifested. He is knowledge, He is the object of knowledge, and He is the goal of knowledge" (13.18). He says that the indwelling Lord is the source of the three modes of nature—goodness, passion, and ignorance—and is thus not affected by them. This Supersoul, says Krishna, is beyond the scope of the material senses (13.13–17). He must be perceived by spiritual means— by transcending the three material modes. I will discuss these modes at greater length later, as the *Gita* merely mentions them here but goes into detail as the text moves on. This important subject (the three modes) was introduced to Arjuna in the *Gita*'s second chapter and is periodically referred to throughout.

Next Krishna describes both the Field and its Knower in a slightly different way, one that brings to bear Arjuna's question about enjoyment: He mentions them as *prakriti* (material nature, consisting of the three modes), of which the body (or the Field) is an extension, and *purusha* (the living entity as an enjoyer, as opposed to as "a knower"). He also discusses a related subject: the cause and nature of the soul's entanglement in the material world. In other words— He discusses the *purusha*'s bondage in the world of *prakriti*

(13.20–24). This bondage is a direct result of wanting to enjoy separately from Krishna.

Again, just as God is the ultimate *kshetra-jna*, or Knower of the Field, He is also the Ultimate Enjoyer, or *purusha*. Thus, our entanglement in material illusion begins when we identify with the body, but, further, when we identify with Him. While we may enjoy material nature, we should remember that our enjoying capacity is limited, and that our primary position is that of God's eternal servant in love and devotion. As the *Gita* says, we are subservient to Him who is "a transcendental enjoyer, the supreme proprietor, who exists as the overseer and permitter" (13.23). As soon as we think we are the ultimate enjoyer, we are bound by material illusion. This bondage, Krishna again insists, can be transcended by realization of the Supersoul.

In the next two verses, He mentions different paths by which such realization can take place—Dhyana, Sankhya, Karma-yoga, and the path of receiving knowledge from authorities (13.25–26). Krishna indicates that the path is not as important as the goal: Supersoul must be realized at all costs.

Chapter 13 concludes by stating that one who can analytically understand the entire material manifestation as a combination of the soul and material elements, and who can see, beyond them, the Supreme Soul (Supersoul), becomes eligible for liberation from the material world.

——— **The *Gita* and Modern Psychology** ———

To understand analytically the accouterments of this world and to see them in relationship to God is the main teaching of this portion of the *Gita.* Apparently, among the many lessons to be learned from the *Gita,* the mind-related teachings of analysis and contemplation have made a particularly powerful impact among Western scholars. Far from being confined to subjects of theology and philosophy, the *Gita* is often thought of as an early source of psychological science, systematically describing the *indriya,* the sense organs (ear, eye, nose, skin, tongue) and the organs of action (larynx, hands, feet, and the components of excretion and procreation), in relation to the mind and the intellect. The *Gita* teaches that these sense organs furnish *manas,* the mind, with impressions of the outer world, and that the mind, in turn, informs the *buddhi,* or intellect. This enables us to doubt, to make decisions, and to transform our will into action. To make this more clear, the *Gita* draws upon imagery used in the ancient *Katha Upanishad:* The body is compared to a chariot being led by five horses (the senses), who have a tendency to run amok. The mind is symbolized by the reins, the driving instrument, and the intelligence, ideally, is the driver. The passenger himself is the soul (*atman*), who is affected by whether the chariot is run by the intellect, the mind, or a pack of wild horses.

While certain schools of behavioral psychology deny the soul, or *atman,* there are many modern branches of progressive psychology that recognize its place in our lives, emphasizing the importance of cultivating a deeper sense of who we are. Ideally, this refers to our real self, not a materially constructed derivative. As the late Karen Horney, famed American psychoanalyst, writes in her essay "Finding the Real Self": "I saw that we *become* neurotic seeking or defending a pseudo-self, a self-system, and we *are* neurotic to the extent that we are self-less" (p. 12). In other words, we must have *some* conception of self but, more importantly, we should have an *accurate* one. The *Gita*'s teaching on this subject has implications that Horney would find interesting. Although I have explored these ideas of self earlier in this book, it would be useful to mention them again in relation to modern psychology.

The *Gita* teaches that our material predicament stems from a false sense of who we are. If we are the body, then, naturally, there are a particular set of activities that go along with that sense of identity. But if we are *not* the body and instead partake of the nature of the spirit, then, just as naturally, there must be a range of activities that accompany this particular perception of self. When one learns to function on this spiritual level, as taught in the *Gita,* he has achieved *yoga*—the natural activity of the soul.

The *Gita* asserts that we have acclimated ourselves, over many births, to the activities of the body, to the point where they feel natural. However, when we practice *yoga,* says Krishna, we gradually remember our true selves, and we feel how much more natural and even blissful soul-related activities can be. We then take on a new perception of our bodies: They are valuable instruments in the Lord's service, but they are not *who we are.*

In Geary J. C. Sheridan's *Vaisnava India,* the "fourth force" of modern psychology, known as transpersonal psychology, is called upon to further emphasize the spiritual nature of the self. Sheridan quotes Dr. Roberto Assagioli, a respected colleague of Freud and Jung, who advises that one practice techniques of creative visualization and guided meditation to achieve self-actualization. These techniques have become a common and even popular part of psychological discourse. Assagioli suggests (in his classic work *The*

Act of Will) that one can begin such meditation by inwardly contemplating the following truths: "I *have* a body, but *I am not* my body. . . . I value my body . . . , but *it is only an instrument*. I treat it well. I seek to keep it in good health, but it is not myself" (p. 214). This directly parallels the fundamental teachings of the *Bhagavad-gita*.

In his technique of guided meditation, Assagioli takes his patients through each step of what the *Gita* would call the beginning of self-realization. He has his patients meditate in the following way: "I have emotions but I am not my emotions." Then, "I have a mind, but I am not my mind" (p. 215). Finally, after meditating for some time on these "mantras," gradually lifting his patients out of the bodily conception of life, he has them contemplate the implications of their meditation:

> What am I then? What remains after having disidentified myself from my body, my sensations, my feelings, my desires, my mind, my actions? It is the essence of myself—a center of pure consciousness. . . . *I affirm my identity with this center* and realize its permanency and its energy. (p. 216)

We may remember that Vance takes Junah through such a guided visualization—an inquiry into the true self—and I quote that section in the introduction to this book. Krishna, of course, has Arjuna go through the same thing, enlightening him as to the nature of the soul. This journey to the real self, it should again be pointed out, is just the beginning of self-realization: As stated earlier, once one properly identifies with who he really is, there is an entire range of activities that are soul-related. It is in exploring this range of activities that the *Gita* really hits its mark.

In their book *Yoga and Psychotherapy*, authors Swami

Rama, Rudolph Ballentine, A. Weinstock, and Swami Ajaya suggest a merger of modern Western psychology and that of the *Gita*. After all, they write, modern psychology focuses on individuals who are ill, while the *Gita* takes those who are well to new heights. In their own words:

> *Yoga* contrasts with modern psychotherapy in that it was not developed as a system for treating the disabled, but rather as a training method for the able. The range of growth that is focused on is different. Psychotherapy concentrates primarily on the areas of growth that lie just before the ego. *Yoga* is interested primarily in development and growth beyond the ego. The training of *yoga* is geared to those who have already worked their way through the more massive attachments to the point of a "dissatisfied normality," those who are searching for avenues of further growth despite the fact that they are, in the eyes of society, well adapted and acceptably productive. (pp. 176–77)

The teachings of *Gita*, it is true, will particularly benefit those who have already penetrated the fundamental illusions of the world, the false conceptions of the self, the false ego, to the point of earnestly seeking a higher reality. But, make no mistake, the *Gita* offers effective psychological guidance for those who are not yet there, who must go a bit further before embracing spiritual life proper. There are teachings in the *Gita* that take one—gradually—from physical to mental, intellectual, and, finally, spiritual levels of existence.

In golf, too, there is a frequently explored gateway from physical to psychological dimensions of the game, often bordering on the spiritual. A plethora of books have recently been released that analyze this subject, for example, Jeff Wallach's *Beyond the Fairway: Zen Lessons, Insights, and Inner Attitudes of Golf,* or Richard Coop and Bill Fields's *Mind Over Golf,* or Patrick J. Cohn's *The Mental Game of Golf.* The list goes on and on. All good books, all implying that *jnana* plays an important role in golf, all suggesting that self-realization can make one a better golfer.

Naturally, golf doesn't necessitate elaborate conceptions of the self (although Vance would probably argue with me here). Nonetheless, mental discipline as well as concentration and awareness are fundamental to a good game. The above books and others like them promote visualization techniques not so much for establishing a golfer's true identity as for "seeing yourself succeed, seeing the shot you want to hit." These books suggest practicing yoga and meditation, lauding these ancient Eastern techniques as reliable methods for attaining the mental equilibrium and focus necessary for becoming accomplished on the golf field. Ben Hogan, golf pro par excellence, has said, "Golf is twenty percent technique and eighty percent mental."

Golf and the inner, mental life have a longstanding relationship. In Canadian writer Arnold Haultain's classic book *The Mystery of Golf,* which was published as long ago as 1908, he explained, in humorous but insightful terms, some possible connections between the mind and the green:

> Golf, indeed, is a fruitful field of psychological phenomena. For example, hypnotists of the most modern school aver, I believe, that there exist somewhere in the brain or mind of man five distinct layers of consciousness. For proofs of multiple consciousness the hypnotist should frequent the links. He will there often find one layer of consciousness roundly upbraiding another, sometimes in the most violent language of abuse, for a foozled stroke; and so earnest sometimes is the vituperation poured by the unmerciful abuser upon the

unfortunate foozler, that truly one is apt sometimes sincerely to commiserate with the former, and to regard him as the victim of a multiple personality, and not at all blameable for his own poor play. Golfers, too, have I known who imagine themselves constantly accompanied by a sort of Socratic daimon prompting them to this, that, or the other method of manipulating the club—without doubt a mystic manner of looking upon one's alter ego. It would be interesting to "suggest" to a duffer, while in the cataleptic trance, to keep his eye on the ball, and to follow through, and then to watch the result. If these fundamental rules (so easy to preach, so difficult to practice) could be relegated to some automatic substratum of consciousness, leaving the higher centres free to judge of distance and direction (for it is thus, probably, that the man who has golfed from childhood plays), the task of many a professional might be simplified. All of which goes to show that, in the game of golf, the mind plays a larger part than, in many quarters, is apt to be imagined. (pp. 15–16)

Haultain writes with a certain style, but his thoughts would be more clearly expressed in terms of the three modes of nature—goodness, passion, and ignorance. He describes competent golfers, angry or abusive ones, and those who are foolish. And these certainly correspond to the three modes, if in a somewhat disorganized way. As we shall see, the *Gita*, in explaining the world in terms of these modes, offers a methodical and far-reaching view of reality.

The Three Modes of Nature

As described in the *Gita*'s thirteenth chapter, the soul is entangled in the material world because of association with the three modes of material nature. In this fourteenth chapter, Krishna explains precisely what the modes of nature are, how they act, and how they bind one to the material world. He also reveals how one can be liberated from their influence.

Krishna begins by telling Arjuna that He will now, again, reveal "this supreme wisdom, the best of all knowledge." By understanding such knowledge one can attain to "the spiritual nature" and attain liberation from the cycle of birth and death (14.1-2). Krishna explains that all living beings take birth within this material world because He places them into the womb of material nature. For this reason, He is the "seed-giving father" of all the different species of life, and the *Gita* makes careful record of this (14.3–4).

With great compassion, He brings His children into the material world, so that they may learn the lessons they need, and, once this is done, return to Him. The material nature into which He brings them consists of three modes: *sattva* (goodness), *rajas* (passion), and *tamas* (ignorance). These modes condition the living entity according to his or her innermost desires (14.5). Briefly, the mode of goodness is characterized by relative purity, illumination, happiness, and freedom from sinful reactions; the mode of passion involves uncontrollable desire and longing, over-endeavor, greed, and attachment to the fruits of one's labor; and the mode of ignorance consists of foolishness, madness, illusion, inertia, indolence, and sleep. Having explained this at some length, Krishna shows how these modes condition and bind the soul according to his individual tastes and needs. Each soul is unique, and so the modes are applied in different ways for each individual. Krishna then describes the fate of differently conditioned souls after death (14.6–18).

From the day I first became aware of the three modes, I

was confident that they could be applied to any sphere of activity. This confidence grew when I began to research golf and related topics for the writing of this book. When I came upon Ralph Seaman's introductory book on golf *Golfers I Know,* I was amazed that, without any apparent knowledge of the *Gita* or the modes of nature, he describes three kinds of golfers who fit into categories defined by the three modes. And unlike Haultain's version, these links are pretty clear:

> There are basically three kinds of golfers, and I like to think of them in terms of white, red, and black (though, in this context, the colors have nothing to do with the races associated with them). The white player is calm and assured. He knows his game. He enjoys it on a simple level, and plays it happily. He's usually a good player. The red golfer is always anxious—he *has* to win. He is often restless and is usually willing to "make it interesting" by betting on the outcome. He's usually someone who is quite good but could be a better golfer if only he would calm down. Finally, the black player is sluggish and uninformed. He seems disinterested and one wonders why he is on the green at all. He makes the game a burden for himself and everyone else. (pp. 29–30)

According to the *Gita,* one can transcend the influence of the three modes and return to one's true spiritual nature by understanding how the modes work and by understanding that Krishna is transcendental to them (14.19). This is similar to Krishna's teaching in the prior chapter that one can free oneself from material life by understanding matter, spirit, and the controller of both—the Supersoul. Here Krishna extends the Field of Action and *prakriti* to include the subtle modes of nature.

When one transcends the modes, as when one realizes one's nature beyond the body and beyond *prakriti,* he attains freedom from the miseries of birth, disease, old age, and death. Accomplishing this spiritual end, one can "enjoy a higher taste even in this life" (14.20). This is an important point. Krishna is not simply making promises for some future life, and in this sense His teaching is not "otherworldly." By understanding how the modes act on people in this world, one can understand their motivations and underlying psychology. Moreover, by studying the modes in one's own life, one will be better able to evaluate one's own idiosyncrasies, gradually transcending the modes altogether. Naturally, this all leads to a more fulfilling, conscious life in this world as well as the next.

To gain a more thorough understanding of the modes, Arjuna asks Krishna three questions: "What are the symptoms of one who has gone beyond the modes of nature?" "How does he behave?" and "How, precisely, does he transcend the modes?" (14.21). In essence, Krishna answers the first two questions as follows: Persons who have transcended the modes of nature, having realized their true essence as spiritual beings—beyond their bodies and in fact beyond all matter—are unconcerned with and unaffected by the actions and reactions of the material world. They are freed from all material dualities, such as pleasure and pain, honor and dishonor, and they do not engage in any fruitive actions. They are concerned for people who have not yet realized these things, and they humbly strive to help them. In answer to Arjuna's third question, Krishna says that one transcends the modes by acting on His behalf—whether it comes in the form of Karma-yoga, Jnana-yoga, or Bhakti-yoga. When one first transcends the modes, Krishna says, one attains to the level of Brahman, the preliminary spiritual position, which is characterized by freedom from material contamination (14.22–26). From this point, one goes on to realize the Lord in the heart and then Bhagavan, Krishna Himself.

In the final verse of the chapter, Krishna explains why realization of Brahman leads to realization of Him: He is the basis or source of Brahman (14.27). In other words, He is Brahman, even if Brahman is only a rudimentary form of His essential nature. Therefore, when one has attained the preliminary spiritual level known as Brahman (which carries with it freedom from the conditioning born of the modes of nature), one becomes qualified to engage in the devotional service of Krishna (the Supreme Brahman).

—————— A Banyan Tree on the Green ——————

The *Gita*'s fifteenth chapter begins by comparing the material world—with its complex network of fruitive activity (*karma*) and entangling results—to an intricately entwined banyan tree, with its roots upward and its branches down. The various parts of the tree (roots, branches, twigs, leaves, and so on) are compared to fruitive activity, piety and impiety, the senses, the sense objects, the results of fruitive activities, the different planetary systems, and so forth. By performing fruitive activities with one's own pleasure in mind, the entangled soul is forced to wander from branch to branch (i.e., from body to body, planet to planet) in the knotty tree of the material world.

It is comparable to hitting a ball into a terrible water hazard, or into the worst sandtrap imaginable. In golfspeak, it's known as "a bunker." And it's like the worst of bunkers, where the ball is positioned in a way that golfers would call "a fried egg." This refers to the most feared shot one can make—a shot that complicates the game immeasurably. A related golf phrase would be "the embedded lie." This is when a ball is positioned in the bank below the lip—you pretty much can't get it out. A simple game made complicated. And that, again, makes the game comparable to the inverted banyan tree known as the material world—life in God's wonderful creation is made more difficult by the assault of the senses, wherein a sincere, well-meaning person becomes the victim of lust, anger, and greed. The hardship of a golfer who hits an embedded lie correlates to the confusion that keeps us here in the material world—our game becomes unnecessarily complex, the simple joy of our true swing becomes weighed down by desire, fear, and anxiety. Or, perhaps a better analogy involves miniature golf—trying to deal with an endlessly complicated obstacle course would be tantamount to the frustration of living in the labyrinthine banyan tree identified with the material world.

The *Gita*'s banyan tree, it should be pointed out, is merely a mirror image, a reflection, of a banyan tree in the spiritual world. It is for this reason that it is described as a tree with its roots growing upward and its branches going down—it is the opposite of that which really exists. The metaphor is meant to illustrate the backwardness of the material world, where the "reality" we see in our day-to-day life is little more than inverted truth. Krishna's teaching, however, gives hope. He declares that "one who knows this banyan tree is the knower of the *Vedas*" (15.1). In other words, the ultimate purpose of Vedic knowledge is to understand this entangling "tree" of the material world and, by such knowledge, extricate oneself from it (15.2). In effect, understanding the complexities of this banyan tree and how it relates to the soul and God has been the main subject of the *Gita* thus far, since Krishna has explained it in several ways using diverse terminology.

Krishna extends the metaphor by elaborating on the means by which one might extricate oneself from the material world: "Using the powerful axe of nonattachment," He says, "one must cut down this banyan tree with determination. Thereafter one must seek that situation from which, having gone, one never comes back" (15.3–4). Krishna then describes the surrendering process and gives a brief description of the spiritual world. He mentions that His realm is self-illuminating and that one who goes there never returns —for such a person, the inverted banyan tree assumes its original form (15.5–6). Thus, instead of just pointing out the dark roots of material complexity, Krishna gives a taste of the sunny destination awaiting the aspiring spiritualist.

In the next few verses, Krishna returns to the subject of the conditioned living entities in the material world and how they are transmigrating from one body to the next. Such living entities, Krishna tells us, are His eternal "fragmental parts." According to the particular mentality of the bound soul, he develops a particular gross material body that is equipped with a particular set of senses. With these, he enjoys a particular set of sense objects. This explains the great variety of species on the planet, and why they are each equipped with a particular sensual forte: the bear sleeps six months at a time, a pigeon is able to have frequent sex. There is a body for each type of pleasure the soul may aspire to. Self-realization, Krishna says, begins when one tires of sensual pleasure and instead desires Him.

Krishna asserts that the foolish or deeply conditioned cannot understand this process of transmigration, but the wise can (15.7–11).

Krishna dedicates the remainder of the chapter to discussing His own supreme nature. He enumerates some of His manifestations in the material world by which He maintains all that exists:

> The splendor of the sun, which dissipates the darkness of the whole world, comes from Me. And the splendor of the moon and the splendor of fire are also from Me. . . . I enter into each planet, and by My energy they stay in orbit. . . . I accompany living beings by situating Myself in everyone's heart, and from Me come their remembrance, knowledge, and forgetfulness. By all the *Vedas* am I to be known; indeed I am the compiler of Vedanta, and I am the only true knower of the *Vedas*. (15.12–20)

Krishna then explains something He had touched on earlier, that there are two classes of beings: the "fallible" (the conditioned souls in the material world) and the "infallible"(the liberated souls in the spiritual world). He is beyond them both, He says, for He maintains the material and spiritual worlds, and all the beings contained therein (15.16–17). Thus He is "celebrated both in the world and in the *Vedas* as that Supreme Person" (15.18). Whoever knows Him as such is "the knower of everything" and, because of this, he engages in undeviating devotional service (15.19). Krishna concludes by declaring that knowledge of His preeminent position and the rendering of service to Him are the essence of what is taught in the Vedic scriptures (15.20). Thus, *jnana* leads to *bhakti;* to know Krishna is to love Him.

"Love Your Enemy"

In the sixteenth chapter, Krishna describes and compares two kinds of qualities and the people who possess them. He first mentions the divine or transcendental (*daiva*) qualities—these are related to the mode of goodness and are conducive to spiritual progress. He then mentions the demoniac (*asura*) qualities. These are related to the modes of passion and ignorance, and, conversely, they are detrimental to spiritual progress. In addition, they lead to lower birth and further material bondage.

Those who possess divine qualities generally live regulated lives, abiding by the authority of scripture, and in this way they attain perfection; those possessing demoniac qualities act whimsically (without reference to spiritual authority) and are bound by material nature. There are of course exceptions to the rule—there are regulated "spiritualists" who are in fact evil and care nothing for their fellow human beings. And there are those who neglect scripture but have a good heart, are well intentioned, and are wise. But, in general, Krishna says that people can be divided into these two broadly defined categories.

To make these two categories clearer, Krishna lists twenty-three transcendental qualities "born of the godly atmosphere" (16.1–3). Some examples: fearlessness, purification of one's existence, charity, self-control, compassion, gentleness, fortitude, cleanliness, modesty, simplicity, forgiveness, and freedom from both envy and the passion for honor. In all, the list reads pretty much like the one in chapter 13, wherein Krishna enumerates qualities that constitute true knowledge.

Krishna then summarizes the qualities of the demoniac—arrogance, pride, anger, conceit, harshness, and ignorance. Krishna states that the transcendental qualities lead to liberation, whereas the demoniac qualities lead to bondage. He assures Arjuna that he need not worry, for he has been "born with transcendental qualities." This is one of several places in the *Gita* where Krishna uses an interesting form of psychology on the mighty bowman. Essentially, He encourages Arjuna by telling him that his involvement in the battle is not demoniac, for he is not acting under the influence of anger, false prestige, or harshness. According to the scriptural injunctions governing the *kshatriya* class, fighting in a religious war is the proper thing to do, whereas refraining from such duty would be demoniac, or irreligious, at least for him (16.4–5).

Arjuna is called upon to do his duty dispassionately and enthusiastically at the same time. That is to say, he must fight the battle with all he has, and yet, as it says in the Bible, he must love his enemy. In other words, he must perform the Art of Work as Krishna has explained it to him. He must transcend duality and realize the meeting of opposites. More importantly, he must see the divine purpose behind his action.

Bagger Vance also shows Junah the wisdom of overcoming duality, of battling a foe and loving him at the same time:

> Therefore, Junah, love your opponents. When I say love, I don't mean hand them the match. I mean contend with them to the death, the way a lion battles a bear, without mercy but with infinite respect. Never belittle an opponent in your mind, rather build him up, for on the plane of the

Self there can be no distinction between your being and his. Be grateful for your opponents' excellence. Applaud their brilliance. For the greatness of the hero is measured by that of his adversaries. In this too the etiquette and honor of golf reflect the Reality of the Field. Those new to the game often cheer an opponent's misfortune, but the player of wisdom who has entered into the soul of the game schools himself to feel and act the opposite. This too is the greatness of the game. (p. 122)

Much earlier in the *Gita* (in the second chapter), Krishna refers to relativity and material duality with a striking example:

The nonpermanent appearance of happiness and distress and their disappearance in due course of time are like the appearance and disappearance of winter and summer. They arise only because of sense perception, and one must learn to tolerate them without being disturbed. (2.14)

Vance also conveys the illusory nature of relativity and materialistic duality:

"'Victory' and 'defeat'"—he spat the words with revulsion, as if their very sound were obscene—"I'm sick to death of them, and of men contending as if there was any difference between them!" (p. 95)

Divine and demoniac are, in a sense, opposite sides of the same coin. One must transcend these dualities and rise not only to the mode of goodness, in which one embodies the divine qualities, but to the level known as Shuddhasattva—the level of pure goodness, which is beyond all dualities of material existence. This is the goal to which the *Gita* hopes to bring its readers.

--------------------- **The Pleasure Seekers** ---------------------

Krishna graphically describes those of the demoniac nature. As one might expect, atheists and materialists who violate scriptural injunctions are among those whom Krishna frowns upon. Actually, He claims His love for them, and that He is equal to all. But He favors His devotee, and His compassion goes out to the demoniac, for these are people who harm themselves and those around them. Such persons, He says, think of the world as having no foundation or purpose, and thus they tend toward whimsical and destructive activities. For them, the ultimate goal of life is gratification of the senses. They are attracted by impermanent, material things. Bound by overwhelming material desires, they obtain money by any means necessary. They are generally conceited, lusty, spiritually complacent, and impudent, and, because their desires are intense, there is no end to their anxiety (16.6–18). Of course, many if not all of us partake in these qualities to some degree. Krishna is pointing out that we should rise beyond these qualities and strive for the divine nature. For, once situated in goodness, we are more apt to grow into transcendence.

The main point Krishna is making here is that of the futility of material enjoyment, which necessarily ends in misery. Vaishnava teachers remind us that there are basically three possible consequences in the quest for selfish pleasure, and they all end in the same way. (1) We seek out pleasure, and it eludes us. This leads to misery. (2) We seek out pleasure, and we achieve it. But it doesn't live up to our expectations. This also leads to misery. (3) We seek out pleasure, we achieve it, and it does, indeed, live up to our expectations. However, we must inevitably lose it after some time. This, too, leads to misery. Is there any approach to pleasure that doesn't end in one of these three ways? Even when we are successful at material enjoyment, it must come to an end after some time. Ultimately, we or our loved ones die, and so, if we are selfishly attached, we suffer. Love and pleasure are, of course, natural. And Krishna does not deny us this. But unless we learn the art of actionless action, or work in God consciousness, we are destined to misery. Therefore, Krishna calls demoniac those forms of life that neglect the development of Krishna consciousness.

Such demoniac persons, He says, "sink down to the most abominable position of existence" and eventually take birth in the lower species of life (16.19–20). For this reason, Krishna cautions, every sane person should give up lust, anger, and greed, the "three gates leading to hell." By escaping these, one can elevate oneself first to goodness and then to self-realization. From there, one may approach the "the supreme destination" (16.21–22).

Krishna concludes by saying that one who is serious about the ultimate goal of life should not live whimsically. For others, they may do as they like, but they will not attain ultimate happiness. In fact, Krishna says, they will suffer in this life and in the next. Rather, one should follow the regulations of scripture (meant to elevate a person to spiritual realization), or intuitively follow their heart—if it leads them to the Lord. Krishna says that the safest path is to follow Vedic scriptural regulations and to guide one's life accordingly. This will gradually lead to spiritual perfection (16.23–24).

──────── **Knowledge Isn't Everything** ────────

The *Gita* next addresses a problem that can arise when one develops spiritual knowledge. As the saying goes, "A little knowledge is a dangerous thing." On the spiritual path, one can develop a tendency to be a tad too creative, at least according to the standards set down in the *Gita*. As the seventeenth chapter opens, Arjuna asks about the legitimacy of constructing one's own method of worship, ignoring scriptural regulations. Krishna has stressed the importance of abiding by traditional scriptures, and Arjuna here wants to be certain that he is understanding Krishna correctly: Does one have to honor the paths set down by the sages, as preserved in scripture, or can one concoct one's own path to truth? Actually, Arjuna phrases the question in relation to what he has just learned about the three modes of nature. He wants to know if finding one's own way to God, without the help of scripture, reflects faith in goodness, passion, or ignorance (17.1).

In response, Krishna explains that there are indeed three types of faith, corresponding to and evolving from the three modes of nature (17.2–6). Krishna seems to want Arjuna to figure this out for himself—He doesn't directly answer the question. Rather, He describes the characteristics of four items—food, sacrifice, austerity, and charity—according to each of the three modes. By categorizing foods in this way, Krishna clarifies the whole concept behind the modes: "Foods in goodness increase the duration of life, purify one's existence, and give strength, health, happiness, and satisfaction. They are sweet, juicy, fattening, and palatable. Foods in the mode of passion are too bitter, sour, salty, pungent, dry, and hot. Such foods cause pain, distress, and disease. Food cooked more than three hours before being eaten, which is tasteless, stale, putrid, decomposed, and unclean, is food liked by people in the mode of ignorance" (17.8–10). Generally, a vegetarian-centered diet is seen as healthful and in the mode of goodness. Meat and various processed foods would be characteristic of passion and ignorance.

Sacrifice, penance, and austerity in the lower modes (ignorance and passion) are performed for selfish, temporary, material benefits, such as the attainment of wealth, honor, and power. Under the influence of such modes, I might give in charity to someone who is less fortunate than I. But I would do so only as an ego boost, or because there is something in it for me. The same acts performed in goodness, however, are executed according to duty and scriptural regulations, without fruitive intentions or only for the purpose of purification and elevation (17.7–22). Such a person is more likely to give in a conscious and selfless manner, thinking about the recipient of one's charity rather than oneself.

In the final verses of this chapter, Krishna explains that acts of sacrifice, austerity, and charity should ultimately be performed for His satisfaction only, for only then do they lead to spiritual advancement. Other selfless works are good too, but they do not lead to the supreme destination. As Krishna explains, by becoming spiritually advanced, one can truly help one's fellow human beings, and this is the topmost goal of one who sees things as they are.

Acts of faith performed without faith in the Supreme and in violation of the scriptures (i.e., in passion and ignorance) yield only impermanent, material results and are therefore not of ultimate value. Worship or faith in the mode of goodness, however, is based on scriptural regulation and performed out of duty. It also purifies the heart of the performer and leads to pure faith and devotion for Krishna (17.23–28). Essentially, then, Krishna's answer to Arjuna's original question is that religion cannot be concocted, for if it is, it will be contaminated by passion and ignorance. Rather, one should honor the sages and the progenitors of religious traditions that are time-tested. The goal is love, not innovative ideas, even if they are spiritual.

Knowledge isn't everything. As the mystic don Juan Matus says in the popular *Teachings of Don Juan: A Yaqui Way of Knowledge,* "Power doesn't lie in knowledge, but, rather, it lies in the kind of knowledge one may have." According to the *Gita,* if knowledge doesn't lead to love of God, it is a dead end. Usually, Vance seems to agree with this, as when he describes love as the best of all possible approaches (pp. 73, 74). At times, however, he seems conflicted: "The Knowing is everything," Bagger Vance said. "It is the Knowing alone that survives the death of the body. You are your Knowing. The Knowing finds the swing and the swing is you . . ." (p. 133). The *Gita* teaches that while knowledge is certainly important, it is not everything, even when it has a capital *K.*

——————— **Surrender to the Swing** ———————

The eighteenth chapter of *Bhagavad-gita* summarizes and concludes the *Gita*'s teachings. Since the *Gita* stresses renunciation of material activities and a concomitant engagement in spiritual elevation, Arjuna, in the first verse, asks

Krishna to explain unequivocally the purpose of renunciation and of the renounced order of life (*sannyasa*). In reply, Krishna reiterates much of His teaching from chapter 3—that renunciation does not mean giving up all action, since this is impossible for the embodied soul. It means, rather, giving up the fruitive mentality behind action and instead performing prescribed duties without attachment to their results. For those who are not renounced, Krishna says, the fruits of action—whether desirable, undesirable, or mixed—accrue after death. On the other hand, for the renounced person who acts out of duty to God, there is no personal reaction at all. God, it is said, "devours the reactions of such a person in His unlimited mouths." The *Gita* thus explains that a wise person learns the art of actionless action, learns how to renounce with a loving heart, and is consequently liberated from the bondage of *karma* (18.2–12).

Krishna then explains how it is possible to act without material reactions. This, of course, is something He has explained throughout the *Gita*, but here He brings in a new dimension by drawing on Sankhya philosophy. According to Sankhya, there are five factors of action—the place of action, the performer, the senses, the endeavor, and the Supersoul. One who thinks himself the only factor in action (not considering the others, especially the Supersoul, the ultimate cause of all action) is in ignorance and becomes entangled by the fruits of his work. But when one acts for God, without personally motivated desires, his actions do not entail material reactions.

Vaishnava teachers compare this to someone who fights for the armed forces, or perhaps to a police officer who is dutifully serving the police force. He is not held accountable if he acts properly and with governmental authorization.

Rather, the government is held responsible, for he is acting on its behalf. In a similar way, one who learns to act for God suffers no material reactions. Krishna thus indicates to Arjuna that if he acts according to His directions, he will not be the actual slayer, nor will he suffer the consequences of killing on the battlefield (18.13–18).

Next, briefly, Krishna returns to a discussion of the modes. He explains how they predominate in different aspects of human psychology. Knowledge, action, workers, intelligence, determination, and happiness can each be divided into three types—according to the three modes. Krishna methodically analyzes these, as He did with food, charity, penance, and austerity in the previous chapter (18.19–40). By analyzing various psychological traits according to the modes, Krishna explains how the four occupational divisions of human society, explained earlier (*brahmanas*, *kshatriyas*, *vaishyas*, and *shudras*), fit into this system: *brahmanas* are in goodness; *kshatriyas* are in a mixture of goodness and passion; *vaishyas* partake of passion and ignorance; and *shudras* are in ignorance.

Krishna next explains that by adhering to the duties prescribed by one's own occupational division and by offering the results of one's work to the Lord, one can attain perfection. By working in accordance with his social duty—which is determined by the modes of nature—the conditioned soul can ultimately transcend the modes. Therefore, it is in Arjuna's best interest to act according to *kshatriya* principles and fight in the battle—it is best for him, it will benefit the world, and it will bring Krishna satisfaction (18.41–48).

Krishna sums up by saying that the highest perfection of renunciation can be attained by control of the mind and by complete detachment from material things and material

enjoyments (18.49). Krishna then explains the stage following renunciation: attainment of Brahman, the preliminary
stage of transcendence. This state, based on spiritual knowledge, is characterized by joyfulness—a product of freedom
from material desire and duality. "In that state," Krishna
says, "one achieves pure devotion unto Me" (18.50–54).
This is no doubt a lofty goal. There are lesser goals that one
could be proud of. Simply functioning in the mode of goodness is something many will never achieve. But Krishna is
concluding His sermon to Arjuna, and in that spirit He is
mentioning the ultimate fruit of spiritual practice.

Along these same lines, Krishna reveals to Arjuna the
decisive conclusion of all His teachings: The ultimate duty of
every living entity is to surrender unto Him in pure, transcendental love and devotion. Only by devotion can
Krishna—the Supreme Absolute Truth, the Personality of
Godhead—be understood. And by understanding Krishna,
one can enter into the kingdom of God (18.55). Acting
always under His supreme protection, always conscious of
Him, His devotee transcends all obstacles of conditional life
and reaches the spiritual kingdom by His grace (18.56–58).

Krishna warns Arjuna that even if he neglects His divine
instructions and, under the influence of illusion, avoids his
duty, he will still be compelled to fight by his conditioning
as a *kshatriya* (18.59-60). He explains to Arjuna that when
one realizes that He (Krishna) is the Supersoul in the heart,
the supreme controller and friend of all living entities, one
naturally surrenders to Him. In Arjuna's case, he should do
the same by fighting this divinely inspired battle. In the end,
he will achieve transcendental peace and attain the eternal
abode (18.61–62).

Krishna allows His words to sink in. He has no intention

of forcing Arjuna's hand. After instructing Arjuna to deliberate on this very esoteric knowledge—and to make up his
own mind—Krishna imparts "the most confidential part of
knowledge," the supreme instruction, the essence and conclusion of the *Gita:*

> Always think of Me, become My devotee, worship Me, and
> offer praises unto Me. By this method you will surely come
> to Me. I promise you this because you are My very dear
> friend. Give up all conceptions of religion and just surrender
> unto Me. I will protect you from all sinful reactions. Do not
> fear, worry, or hesitate. (18.63–66)

In other words, one should ideally abandon all preliminary religious processes and duties—such as Karma-yoga,
Jnana-yoga, Dhyana-yoga, the socioreligious duties of the
social orders, attainment of Brahman and Paramatma, and
so on, noble as they are—and simply surrender unto Him as
His pure devotee. This is known as the "supreme verse," or
the "ultimate instruction," of the *Gita.* After enlightening
Arjuna about so many paths and possible avenues to truth,
He tells him that the essence of it all is to surrender to Him
in love and devotion. Vance expresses his own version of
Gita 18.66, quoted above: "I will never abandon you. No sin,
no lapse, no crime however heinous can make me desert
you, nor yield up to you any less than my ultimate fidelity
and love" (p. 186).

In the next verse, Krishna states the qualifications for
understanding the *Gita:* The hearer must be austere,
devoted, nonenvious, and engaged in Krishna's service
(18.67). One who imparts Krishna's teachings is Krishna's
most dear servant and attains pure devotion to Him (18.68–
69). One who studies the *Gita,* it is said, "worships Krishna

by his intelligence," and one who hears its teachings with faith is freed from all sins (18.70-71).

To show the world that Arjuna benefited from Krishna's instruction, the Lord asks of Arjuna, "Have you heard this with your mind at perfect attention? And are your ignorance and illusion now dispelled?" Arjuna confidently answers, "My dear Krishna, O infallible one, my illusion has dissipated and I have regained my memory by Your grace. I have now regained composure and I am free from doubt. I am prepared to act according to Your instructions" (18.72–73).

 The *Gita* concludes:

> Wherever there is Krishna, the master of all mystics, and wherever there is Arjuna, the supreme archer, there will also be opulence, victory, extraordinary power, and morality. That is my opinion. (18.74–78)

This reassuring sentiment is also expressed in *Bagger Vance:*

> "Don't be afraid, Hardy," [said Junah]. "Whatever Vance is, he will never harm you. In fact, I'll make you a promise: As long as he stands beside you, no harm can come to you from any quarter." (p. 143)

Endgame
Or,
How Does All of This Apply to Me?

Thus have I explained to you the most confidential aspects of knowledge and truth. Fully deliberate on everything I have told you, and then do what you wish to do.

—*Bhagavad-gita* 18.83

There is much that one can learn from both the *Gita* and *Bagger Vance.* Among the most important of these lessons is that of doing one's duty. This is accompanied by an equally important teaching: Walking away from a difficult situation does not make that situation go away. To avoid duty is not a solution. Psychiatrist M. Scott Peck might as well have been thinking of Junah or his alter ego, Arjuna, when he wrote the following in *The Road Less Travelled:*

> We cannot solve life's problems except by solving them. This statement may seem idiotically tautological or self-evident, yet it is seemingly beyond the comprehension of much of the human race. This is because we must accept responsibility for a problem before we can solve it. We cannot solve a problem by saying "It's not my problem." We cannot solve a problem by hoping that someone else will solve it for us. I can solve a problem only when I say, "This is my problem

and it's up to me to solve it." But many, so many, seek to avoid the pain of their problems by saying to themselves: "This problem was caused me by other people, or by social circumstances beyond my control, and therefore it is up to other people, to society, to solve this problem for me. It is not really my personal problem." (p. 32)

As the *Gita* begins, Arjuna tries to avoid a responsibility that is clearly his. Because he acts in this way, Krishna is able to teach him the importance of doing the right thing— a lesson from which we can all benefit. He also teaches Arjuna to think deeply about who he is: Is he the body or is he the life force within the body? No one can analyze this for us. We must do this on our own. What is our own Authentic Swing, and how should we pursue it in this life? Both the *Gita* and *Bagger Vance* ask us to ponder these questions.

In other words, these books ask us to consider our course of action based on who we are. As stated previously, if we think we are the body, then we will necessarily act in a particular way. And if we identify with the soul, we will act in another way. Once we determine whether we are body or soul, we must then discover the most appropriate outlet for that realization—the course of action that suits our psychophysical makeup best. At all costs, we should be determined to find out what is true and to live by it.

Scott Peck, as a qualified specialist who has thoroughly analyzed the human condition, tells us that living a life based on truth is fundamental and that the virtues of such living should be obvious. Truth, he says, is reality. And unless we see things as they are, we will not be able to properly function in the real world. Thus, the more clearly we see the reality of day-to-day life, the better equipped we are to deal with it. The converse is also true: If we do not clearly see the world the way it actually is, we are less likely to deal with it appropriately—we are victimized by misperception and illusion. According to Peck (and the *Gita* as well), this is the case for most of us. Consequently, modern people are generally unable to ascertain the correct course of action and to make reasonable decisions for long-term happiness. Along these lines, Peck tells us that our view of reality is like a map with which to negotiate the terrain of life. If the map is clear and accurate, we will experience the calm of certainty—we will generally know where we are, and, if we have decided where we want to go, we will know how to get there. If the map is false and inaccurate, we will be lost.

This is the premise of the *Gita*. But the *Gita* goes further, giving direction and guidance for breaking free of illusion. According to the *Gita,* one needs discipline. Modern life bombards us with one dulling sensation after the next, and to rise beyond it, to become peaceful, one must learn to quiet the mind. Krishna recommends *yoga.* This brings us out of the illusions associated with day-to-day life and establishes us in the Self. From that point, seeing things as they are, we have a chance to become situated in reality.

Many, however, have become accustomed to their "old way" of doing things. They avoid change, even if it is for their benefit. This is called conditioning. Both Arjuna and Junah, by their own reactions to their respective situations, show us the misery and frustration associated with such conditioning. But they can't seem to help it. Their conditioned responses leave them in a lurch, and if not for Krishna and Vance, they would remain in their tortured state. By the grace of their saviors, they embark on "the road less travelled," as Scott Peck would say, the road of self-examination and dedication to the truth.

However, most people, says Peck, will not want to make this effort. By the end of adolescence, we tend to become spiritually and emotionally lazy, unwilling to change deep-rooted habits and conditioned responses to the external world. Gradually, we start to think we know it all. Ironically, our "maps," at this point, are still small and sketchy. We are certain that we know real from unreal, but our view of the world is often narrow and misleading. Overpowered by this inner certainty that our maps are complete and that our worldview is beyond challenge, we begin to shun new information, or, rather, we fear it. Peck tells us that only a fortunate few continue exploring the mystery of reality until the moment of death, ever enlarging and redefining their understanding of the world and what is true and real.

If we are open to new information, as is often the case when we read the *Gita* or *Bagger Vance* for the first time, we experience exhilaration but also pain. The exhilaration comes from an innocent and honest place deep within—we are thrilled at the opportunity to reach for something new and valuable, for our long-awaited introduction to a separate reality. But the pain, again, comes from conditioning. We are being ripped away from that to which we have grown accustomed, from a worldview in which we've invested so much. The process of revising long-cherished beliefs can be devastating. So much is this the case, that it is not uncommon for one to deny the veracity of the new reality with which he or she is faced. Again, Scott Peck offers valuable insight:

What happens when one has striven long and hard to develop a working view of the world, a seemingly useful, workable map, and then is confronted with new information suggesting that that view is wrong and the map needs to be largely redrawn? The painful effort required seems frightening, almost overwhelming. What we do more often than not, and usually unconsciously, is to ignore the new information.

We may denounce the new information as false, dangerous, heretical, the work of the devil. We may actually crusade against it, and even attempt to manipulate the world so as to make it conform to our view of reality. Rather than try to change the map, an individual may try to destroy the new reality. Sadly, such a person may expend much more energy ultimately in defending an outmoded view of the world than would have been required to revise and correct it in the first place. (pp. 45–46)

It is not for us to say which information is right or wrong, or exactly in which direction a person should go. If the *Gita* and *Bagger Vance*—or this book, for that matter—merely serves to provoke thought, that is enough. The inner search may be painful, but it is necessary, and it gets easier as one goes along. Peck agrees. He says that examination of the external world is always less painful than examining the world within. And because this is so, the majority tend to avoid the inner search. Nonetheless, Peck affirms in *The Road Less Travelled* that for one fully dedicated to the pursuit of truth, the pain of inner inquiry is surpassed by the pleasure of knowledge. The pain seems relatively unimportant, he says, and gets less and less so the further one proceeds on the path of self-examination. And because it gets progressively less important, it gets less and less painful. *Bhagavad-gita* adds that when one passes a certain point, the inner search actually becomes blissful. Though it tastes like poison in the beginning, says the *Gita,* it is like nectar in the end.

—————————————— **God and Golf** ——————————————

Throughout this work, I have shown connections not only between the *Gita* and *Bagger Vance* but between general principles of spirituality and psychology, and golf. Since we seem to have latched on to Scott Peck and his insights about reality and self-realization, let us continue by drawing on his recent book, *Golf and the Spirit: Lessons for the Journey,* in which he tells a religious joke concerning golf—a joke that I will tell in my own way.

The joke begins by describing a man and his attachment to the game. He's an excellent player but becomes obsessed, so much so that he neglects his job, his family, and his spiritual life. As the joke goes, the man eventually died and went to Hell. Once there, he meets the devil, an urbane-looking fellow in slacks and a smart sports coat. "Welcome to Hell," the devil said to the golfer, almost making him comfortable. "Our goal here in Hell is to make your stay pleasant. So don't hesitate to call on us for anything—my entire staff is at your disposal."

Hell for this golfer did not conform to his preconceived notions. He was surprised at how pleasing his initial experience was. This gave him a sort of confidence that Hell may not be what most people think it is, and, as he grew accustomed to his surroundings, he asked the devil if there might not be a golf course down here.

"Golf course?" the devil asked. "Certainly. We have the best golf courses in the universe. Take your pick." The devil led him off to what could only be described as a magnificent southern plantation, with four eighteen-hole courses going off in each direction—a north course, a south course, a west course, and an east course—all perfectly trapped and man-icured to deliver the best game possible.

Almost fainting in ecstasy, the golfer now inquired about irons—"You don't have quality golf clubs down here, do you?"

"Clubs?" the devil responded. "We certainly do. Actually, we have the most exquisitely balanced clubs imaginable. Come with me. I'll show you where they are, and you can have your pick."

And so the devil took him to a magnificent clubhouse. The golfer tried a few, and found the perfect club, better than any he had ever used. The devil then introduced him to a group of young boys, each of whom was anxious to caddy. Forgetting he was in Hell, the golfer became thrilled at the prospect of playing a round or two with the devil. The two men approached the field with their clubs and the best of caddies. "Now," said the golfer, "if you would just give me the ball, I will begin."

"Ball?" the devil asked with a wicked smile. "We don't have any balls here. That's what makes it hell."

The joke is a virtual commentary on the *Gita*. Briefly, the golfer's single-minded attachment to the game is what led him down the royal road to hell—he neglected job, family, and religious obligation because he was so clouded by a pleasurable sensation, that is, by his conditioned response to what is, after all, only a game. The *Gita* teaches that we,

– 158 –

too, are so engrossed in the senses and their objects that we fail to see what is truly important: We lose track of our own spiritual dimension and of our own inescapable source, God.

While in Hell, the golfer resumes his attachment, and, as his conditioning increases and he becomes more and more comfortable with his surroundings, he actually comes to like life down there. The *Gita* acknowledges the pleasure that comes from contact of the senses and their objects, but it asserts that spiritual pleasure is even more tangible, and that the material variety pales by comparison. Spiritual pleasure, says the *Gita*, is everlasting and indescribably intense, while material pleasure is temporary and limited.

This temporary, limited nature of the material world relates to the last point of the joke: The *Gita* teaches that in this world, there is always something missing. The world may offer most of what we need—as the golfer had someone with whom to play, a magnificent golf course, the best clubs in the universe, attentive caddies, and so on—but it cannot, by its very nature, offer everything. The balls are missing. What are those balls? Two examples might be lasting happiness and eternality. Because the soul is by nature blissful, we are pleasure seekers; because the soul is eternal, we don't want to die. Misery and temporality are unnatural to the soul, and deep down we know that. And because of this, we resist unhappiness and death. But we are thwarted: Material pleasure leads to suffering, and the body must die. This may seem like a sort of sour-grapes philosophy. But the *Gita* doesn't leave us there. It teaches us how to get in touch with our higher spiritual nature, and in so doing experience transcendent pleasure and immortality.

Golf Course *Ex Nihilo*

Admittedly, words like "transcendent pleasure" and "immortality" can be a bit off-putting. Without a deep understanding of the *Gita,* or, for that matter, spirituality in general, such words and concepts seem rather pie in the sky. I know that I, for one, used to think so, and there is no reason to assume that others would not think in a similar way. Before I close, then, I would like to explain the basic religious contention, at least as I have reasoned it out in my own life. It should be underlined that there are as many reasons to believe as there are to disbelieve, and I am not passing judgment in any case. But I suspect that understanding just why some people choose to believe in things like eternal happiness, immortality, God—indeed, why some believe in a whole spiritual realm—would be interesting to readers of books such as the *Gita* or *Bagger Vance.* It would also be interesting, I am sure, to discover that spiritual belief is often based on reason; this is certainly the case in my own approach to spirituality.

Contemporary society, with its emphasis on science and technology, views itself as being rooted in reason rather than in faith, a word that is often associated with blindly believing in something that is unprovable. Faith, to most people, seems to be at odds with the "scientific method." If we are to be certain about our conclusions, we should base them only on that which we can observe and verify by our own powers of perception. Although this approach seems rational, it has two inherent and major defects (as pointed out in the *Gita*): our sense perception is imperfect and limited. Consequently, even if we take extreme care to reduce our errors of observation, we still perceive only a limited range of phenomena. In addition, even when relying on our own senses, we are forced to admit dependence on belief—or, to use the spiritual word, on faith. Let us look at that a little more closely.

All people want to learn about themselves and the world around them. In this pursuit, most of us accept as evidence only that which we can perceive directly with our senses. But the question arises, How much can we believe our senses? How much faith can we place in them? For example, we see the sun as a little yellow ball in the sky, but, gradually, we learn that it is not. We see our reflection in the mirror, but we soon learn the difference between our body and the image in front of us. Yet, in general, we believe what we see. Our decision to accept sense perception as evidence is therefore in itself a kind of faith.

As already stated, the weaknesses of this kind of faith are twofold. First of all, our senses are imperfect. Our observations will never be exactly correct, a point that has been proven scientifically in Heisenberg's famous uncertainty principle. Thus, conclusions drawn from such imperfect perceptions will necessarily be imperfect in a commensurate way. The second failing of our senses, however, is much more serious: there is a vast range of phenomena that we cannot perceive with our senses at all. For example, as human beings, we are unable to hear certain portions of the known vibratory spectrum. We are sensitive to sound waves of 1,000 to 4,000 cycles per second (cps), but those which exceed 20,000 cps elude us. Dogs and cats can hear up to 60,000 cps, while mice, bats, whales, and dolphins can emit and receive sounds well over 100,000 cps.

A more thought-provoking example of something we are not able to perceive is the past. That which occurred before our birth—before our present set of observations began—cannot possibly become known to us through direct sense perception. Yet we are aware of history, and to declare that there was no past simply because we did not directly perceive it would be the height of arrogance and absurdity. Rather, we firmly believe in the concept of a past, even though much of it is beyond our experience.

In many cases, then, necessity forces us to expand our belief system to accommodate that which lies beyond our own sense perception. We must accept the authority of those who have thoroughly researched a given subject, having faith that they have indeed done so in a competent and accurate way. This is where things get a bit uncertain, or uncomfortable, because we now find ourselves having faith not only in our own sense perception but also in evidence given by others. Sometimes, there is no way around this. For example, to gain knowledge about ancient Indian civilization, no contemporary source will do. For the most part, we would have to explore archaeological remains and the literature of those who lived in India's past, who had the foresight to write things down. This means studying ancient and often complex languages. As if this weren't enough, we have to then decide whether these writings are describing fact or fiction. Here we have strayed onto difficult ground. Nevertheless, as a society we tend to accept such evidence. We even write books of "history" based on our findings and teach them with passion to our young ones.

To better understand the limits of sense perception, let us consider the hypothetical case of a prehistoric cave dweller magically appearing in the middle of an elaborate, contemporary American golf course. Considering the carefully cultivated sod, the neatly manicured green, and the various golf tees he sees around him, the cave man will naturally think about its origin, about how the golf course came to be. It is not overgrown and wild like the terrain to which he is accustomed. He might find the place too magnificent to have been constructed by mere mortals, and so he may assume that it was the direct creation of some powerful spiritual force. He might also consider the possibility that it was always there, like some naturally occurring mountain range. Or he may simply become bewildered and frightened and avoid any real systematic thought on the subject.

On the other hand, a European gentleman mystically placed on the American green will, even on a first visit, have no difficulty in understanding that it was designed and built by many workers and craftsmen. Although our cultured visitor did not see the golf course being constructed and has not met any of the architects or builders involved, no one will be able to convince him that the putting range has come about in any other way. His belief will be entirely reasonable, but he will have to admit that, strictly speaking, it is a type of faith, albeit an entirely *reasonable faith*.

The conclusion of the cave dweller, however, must be described as *unreasonable faith*. Thus we see that the two words "faith" and "reason" are not opposites, as we sometimes assume, but rather are interdependent concepts. We may be safe in having reasonable faith, such as the faith that a huge golf course has been built by intelligent craftsmen, but we must be cautious of unreasonable faith, or faith based only on superficial thinking and superstition.

Let us go further. Suppose that, upon arriving on the fairway, the European gentleman meets an eccentric-looking fellow who tells him that the golf course was not constructed in any of the previously mentioned ways. Rather, he says that there was an explosion some years back in the general region of the golf course. After the smoke cleared, the entire playing field—complete with fairway, rough, and colorful flags jutting out of eighteen strategically placed holes—was standing in place. All of it—the rolling green and artificial hazards (bunkers and traps), along with the usual accouterments of the game—appeared out of nowhere, *ex nihilo.* Although the European could not, by direct sense perception, prove this doctrine false (since he had not personally observed the construction of the golf course), he will nonetheless conclude that the young man's theory has more holes than the golf course.

What does all this have to do with my belief in God? From scientific observation we learn that the physical structure of a living cell is more complex than the most intricate of golf courses and that the human body has more than thirty trillion of these cells. Furthermore, unlike most links, the human body works smoothly and with amazing precision. Even more amazing, these complex cells have the ability to regenerate themselves—something that golf courses could never do.

This is the point: If we were to conclude that the human body has also been planned and constructed by some highly intelligent person or persons, then we would be possessed of what might be called *reasonable faith.* Nonetheless, there are many in the scientific community who propose that the human body originates from a chance combination of molecules originally set into motion by some tremendous explosion. In my view, such a theory, even if couched in scientific jargon, can only be compared to that of the strange eccentric who claimed that the golf course arose from a nearby explosion. One may charitably call such a hypothesis *unreasonable faith.*

Therefore, the basic contention of theism—that this highly complex universe has been conceived of and constructed by a highly intelligent being—is reasonable. Although we may call it a conclusion based on faith, it is based on an altogether reasonable faith.

Someone may at this point object, saying that although we may verify beyond a reasonable doubt that a golf course was designed and fashioned by intelligent people, we cannot use the same method to verify our conclusion that the universe has been designed and fashioned by a Supreme Being. By way of reply, I would say that few will take the trouble to verify that the links were built in that way, because it is a self-evident fact that does not require verification. Yet, if one really wants to know for sure, one can research the city's records at length, have faith in the words of older citizens who may have themselves witnessed parts of the construction, and corroborate reputable facts.

In much the same way, I have found that God's existence may also, in a sense, be verified, even if few will take the trouble to seek verification. Most choose, instead, to accept on faith the prevailing idea that belief in God is unreasonable. But by the scientific practice of *yoga* as outlined in *Bhagavad-gita,* God's existence can be verified, just as by experimentation we can verify physical laws. The difficulty, again, is only in our unwillingness to conduct the experiment. This harks back to Scott Peck's theory of change: It is painful to redraw the map of our lives, to drastically restructure a worldview in which we have invested so much time and energy.

Modern society has drifted toward the assumption that God does not exist, or that, if He does, His existence is of no real significance in our practical day-to-day lives. As rationalists, we do not find it possible to take seriously a Being we cannot directly perceive with our senses, because to accept such a Being would require a commitment of faith. But in fact every conclusion we come to requires faith, even if it is the simple faith that our sense perception is accurate. The real task, then, is to discriminate between reasonable faith and unreasonable faith.

Since, as I have shown, we can have reasonable faith that this universe and its contents, including ourselves, are the creation of an eminently intelligent and powerful Being, it is inconsistent and illogical to conclude that this Being no longer has any relevance in our lives. Instead, it would seem clear that we should apply considerable thought to the task of better understanding who this Being is, what the nature of His existence is, how He has come to create this universe (and ourselves), what continuing interest He may have in His creations, what our relationship with Him is, what our residual obligations to Him are, and a host of other relevant inquiries that His existence naturally raises. These are dealt with in all religious scriptures, especially *Bhagavad-gita.* No wonder, therefore, that Albert Einstein was once quoted as saying, "When I read the *Gita,* I am prompted to ask myself how God created the universe. Everything else appears to be superfluous." Or, as Michael Murphy writes in *Golf in the Kingdom,* "When I hear *Hare Krishna* on the streets of the city, I hear my own impulse to surrender forever to the One beyond all these incertitudes" (p. 209).

──────────── **A Hopeful Message** ────────────

We may recall the Scott Peck joke related earlier in which an obsessed golfer goes to Hell and finds everything he needs— except golf balls. I offered some suggestions as to just what those balls might be. But it should be clear that the ultimate missing ball is God, for if anything (or anyone) is absent from Hell it is Him. Along these lines, the Vaishnava tradition asserts that if God is missing from our lives, we will, sooner or later, feel incomplete, as if in Hell. Vaishnava sages express this in the following way: We are like adopted children who one day feel a compelling urge to search out our roots. Without knowing our essential origin, we feel unfinished. If we do not explore our source, we can never know closure. At the risk of seeming preachy, then, Vaishnavas tell us that a world divorced from God is a world that is empty. And a world that is empty is a difficult one in which to live.

Not everyone feels this way, Vaishnavas admit. Some lead fulfilling lives without considering their source. Such people, too, will find that the *Gita* contains valuable lessons and thought-provoking ideas. It is a book that serves its readers well, whether or not one approaches it with a longing for God or merely a longing for knowledge. In other words, the *Gita* has a great deal to offer theist and atheist alike, as does *The Legend of Bagger Vance.* This is so because truth is useful and edifying, however one comes to it. Whatever one's background or belief (or nonbelief), if one gives faithful aural reception to abiding reality, one will necessarily benefit from it. As I have shown, there is enough in the way of psychology, sociology, philosophy, ethics, culture, and so on, to make the *Gita* more than a worthwhile read, and, for this reason, it doesn't need to shove God down anyone's throat. To quote Scott Peck yet again in *Golf and the Spirit:*

> Now, it is not my intention, on the last hole of the round, to cram God down anyone's throat. I dislike vomit, and only vomit would be the result of an attempt to do so. With but a few caveats, I am a deep believer in the First Amendment to the U.S. Constitution, which provides for the free exercise of religion. What that amendment means, among other things, is that not only are we free to believe in whatever kind of God we choose, but we are also free to not believe: to have no truck whatsoever with any notion of divinity. The amendment accepts, even encourages, religious diversity.
>
> But why is there such diversity? The basic reason, I suspect, is mystery—and the different ways we handle mystery. For some of us life is such a mysterious business that we have difficulty handling it without resorting to notions of the divine. For others the behavior of God is so mysterious that we have difficulty handling the facts without discounting notions of divinity altogether. And some of us fall in between.
>
> Perhaps the only intellectual sin is to proclaim that there is no mystery at all. Few serious golfers have been guilty of it. In the best compendiums of quotes about golf that I know, appreciation for the mystery of the game is the predominant theme. (p. 292)

Here again is where the *Gita* and *Bagger Vance* meet. Both ask us to ponder the mysteries of life, regardless of our theological outlook. In doing so, there is no loss, only gain. Whatever knowledge we gather in our sojourn through life is to our advantage. And if, in the end, we find that there *is* a God, it is not too late. For a loving God will always accept us, and welcome us in. As Murphy affirms in *Golf in the Kingdom:*

> The world is a passage back to God, that is the only reason it is here.
>
> "Hardest matter is consciousness going back, breaking all the bonds as it has for a billion years." The story of our science is the story of a mutilated vision, said Shivas Irons [the protagonist of Murphy's book]. On one of his charts there was a list of "men who knew," a mind-boggling list running from Pythagoras and Plotinus to Einstein and Henry Ford. It was the crooked golden river of true knowledge running fitfully through our Western centuries. Its title was DANGER-OUS CONNECTIONS. The impression you got when you looked at it for awhile was that the wires joining our world to God were hopelessly tangled. But at the very bottom there was one hopeful sentence, written in tiny letters: "There is still time," it said. (p. 192)

Select Bibliography

Arnold, Bob. *The Meditative Golfer.* New York: Prize Books, 1994.

Assagioli, Roberto. *The Act of Will.* Baltimore, Md.: Penguin Books, 1973.

Barkow, Al, David Barrett, and Ken Janke. *Wit & Wisdom of Golf: Insightful Truths and Bad Lies.* Lincolnwood, Ill.: Publications International, LTD., 1998.

Brahmacari, Subhananda Dasa, ed. *Teaching and Study Guide to Bhagavad-gita As It Is.* Los Angeles, Calif.: Bhaktivedanta Book Trust, 1977.

Braunstein, Mark Mathew. *Radical Vegetarianism.* Los Angeles, Calif.: Panjandrum Books, 1981.

Castañeda, Carlos. *The Teachings of Don Juan: A Yaqui Way of Knowledge.* Reprint. New York: Washington Square Press, 1998.

Cohn, Patrick J. *The Mental Game of Golf.* South Bend, Ind.: Diamond Communications, 1997.

Coop, Richard, and Bill Fields. *Mind Over Golf.* New York: Macmillan, 1993.

Dasa, Bhurijana. *"Surrender Unto Me": An Overview of the Bhagavad-gita.* Vrindavan, India: VIHE Publications, 1997.

Dasa, Drutakarma. "Science, the Bomb, and the Bhagavad-gita." *Back to Godhead Magazine* 22, nos. 2–3 (February–March 1987): 27–29.

Deadwyler, William. "The Contribution of Bhagavata-Dharma Toward a 'Scientific Religion' and a 'Religious Science.'" In *The Synthesis of Science and Religion,* edited by T. D. Singh. San Francisco: Bhaktivedanta Institute, 1987.

Dharma, Krishna. *Mahabharata: The Greatest Spiritual Epic of All Time*. Badger, Calif.: Torchlight Publishing, 1999.

Dimock, Edward C. *Mr. Dimock Explores the Mysteries of the East: Journeys in India*. Chapel Hill, N.C.: Algonquin Books, 1999.

Gandhi, M. K. *M. K. Gandhi Interprets The Bhagavadgita*. New Delhi: Orient Paperbacks, n.d.

Goswami, Srila Bhakti Raksaka Sridhara Deva. *Srimad Bhagavad-Gita: The Hidden Treasure of the Sweet Absolute*. Nadiya, West Bengal: Sri Chaitanya Saraswat Math, 1985.

Griesser, Jean. *God's Song*. Fremont, Calif.: Jain Publishing Company, 1999.

Haultain, Arnold. *The Mystery of Golf*. Reprint. New York: Serendipity Press, 1965.

Herman, A. L. *A Brief Introduction to Hinduism*. Boulder, Colo.: Westview Press, 1991.

Hirst, Jacqueline. "Upholding the World: Dharma in the Bhagavadgita." In *The Fruits of our Desiring: An Enquiry into the Ethics of the Bhagavadgita for our Times*, edited by Julius Lipner. Calgary, Canada: Bayeux Arts, 1997.

Horney, Karen. "Finding the Real Self." *American Journal of Psychoanalysis* 9, no. 1 (1949).

Kapoor, Jagdish Chander. *Bhagavad-Gita: An International Bibliography of 1787–1979 Imprints*. New York: Garland Publishing Company, 1983.

Linder, Mike. *Play It As It Lies: Golf and the Spiritual Life*. Louisville, Ky.: Westminster John Knox Press, 1996.

Loeffelbein, Bob. *Offbeat Golf*. Santa Monica, Calif.: Santa Monica Press, 1998.

Maharaj, B. P. Tirtha. *Srimad Bhagavad-Gita*. Calcutta: Gaudiya Mission, 1948.

Maharaj, Bhakti Prajnan Yati. *Gita Darshan as Bhakti Yoga: As a Chaitanyite Reads It*. Reprint. Madras: Sree Gaudiya Math, 1987.

Maharaja, Srila Jayatirtha. "Can Faith be Reasonable?" *Back to Godhead Magazine* 14, no. 8 (1979).

Maharaja, Sri Srimad Bhaktivedanta Narayana. *The Essence of Bhagavad-gita*. Mathura, U.P., India: Gaudiya Vedanta Publications, 2000.

——. *Srimad Bhagavad-Gita*. Mathura, U.P., India: Gaudiya Vedanta Samiti, 2000.

Miller, Barbara Stoler, trans. *The Bhagavad-Gita: Krishna's Counsel in Time of War*. New York: Bantam Books, 1986.

Miller, Larry. *Beyond Golf*. Walpole, N.H.: Stillpoint Publishers, 1996.

Murphy, Michael. *Golf in the Kingdom*. Reprint. New York: Penguin Putnam, Inc., 1997.

O'Connell, Joseph T. "Caitanya's followers and the Bhagavad-gita: A Case study in Bhakti and the Secular." In *Hinduism: New Essays in the History of Religions,* edited by Bardwell L. Smith, 33–52. Leiden: E. J. Brill, 1976.

O'Flaherty, Wendy Doniger. *The Origins of Evil in Hindu Mythology*. Los Angeles: University of California Press, 1976.

Ollstein, B. W. *Combat Golf*. New York: Viking, 1996.

Peck, M. Scott. *Golf and the Spirit: Lessons for the Journey*. New York: Harmony Books, 1999.

——. *The Road Less Travelled*. New York: Simon & Schuster, 1978.

——. *The Road Less Travelled and Beyond*. New York: Simon & Schuster, 1997.

Prabhavananda, Swami, and Christopher Isherwood. *Bhagavad Gita: The Song of God*. Reprint. Hollywood: Vedanta Press, 1987.

Prabhupada, A. C. Bhaktivedanta Swami. *Bhagavad-gita As It Is*. Reprint. New York: Macmillan, 1972. See 1968 edition for Thomas Merton's foreword, an essay entitled "The Significance of the *Bhagavad-gita*."

——. *Sri Isopanisad*. Reprint. Los Angeles: Bhaktivedanta Book Trust, 1997.

Pressfield, Steven. *The Legend of Bagger Vance: A Novel of Golf and the Game of Life*. Reprint. New York: Avon Books, 1999.

Rama, Swami, Rudolph Ballentine, A. Weinstock, and Swami Ajaya. *Yoga and Psychotherapy: The Evolution of Consciousness*. Reprint. Honesville, Pa.: Himalayan Institute, 1998.

Rosen, Steven J. *Diet for Transcendence: Vegetarianism and the World Religions*. Badger, Calif.: Torchlight Publishing, 1997.

——. *India's Spiritual Renaissance: The Life and Times of Lord Chaitanya*. New York: FOLK Books, 1988.

————. *The Reincarnation Controversy: Uncovering the Truth in the World Religions.* Badger, Calif.: Torchlight Publishing, 1997.

Rosen, Steven J., ed. *Vaisnavism: Contemporary Scholars Discuss the Gaudiya Tradition.* New York: FOLK Books, 1992. Reprint. Delhi: Motilal Banarsidass, 1994.

Seaman, Ralph. *Golfers I Know.* New York: Benaedrum Publishing, 1974.

Sharma, Arvind. *The Hindu Gita: Ancient and Classical Interpretations of the Bhagavadgita.* La Salle, Ill.: Open Court, 1986.

Sharpe, Eric J. *The Universal Gita.* La Salle, Ill.: Open Court, 1985.

Sheridan, Geary J. C. *Vaisnava India.* Malibu Beach, Calif.: Vedic Heritage Foundation, 1994.

Shorto, Russell. *Saints and Madmen: Psychiatry Opens Its Doors to Religion.* New York: Henry Holt, 1999.

Siegel, Lee. *Sacred and Profane Dimensions of Love in Indian Traditions as Exemplified in the Gitagovinda of Jayadeva.* Delhi: Oxford University Press, 1978.

Single, Ted. *The Ultimate Moment.* San Francisco: Lucid Publications, 1980.

Smith, Huston. *The World's Religions.* Reprint. San Francisco: HarperCollins, 1991.

Stark, Abe. *The Love of the Game.* San Francisco: Links Press, 1999.

Trivedi, Mark. *Mohandas Gandhi: The Man and His Vision.* Calcutta: Time Publications, 1968.

Updike, John. *Golf Dreams.* New York: Alfred A. Knopf, 1996.

Vidich, Andrew. *Love Is a Secret: The Mystic Quest for Divine Love.* Boulder Creek, Calif.: Aslan Publishing, 1990.

Wallach, Jeff. *Beyond the Fairway: Zen Lessons, Insights, and Inner Attitudes of Golf.* New York: Bantam Books, 1995.

Zaehner, R. C. *The Bhagavad-gita.* Oxford: Clarendon Press, 1969.

————. *Hinduism.* Reprint. Oxford: Oxford University Press, 1966.

Index